Your friend,

Michael Ellerman

The Insider's Guide to Saving Money

Michael Ellenbogen

Note for Librarians: A cataloguing record for this book is available from Library and Archives Canada at www.collectionscanada.ca/amicus/index-e.html

ISBN 1-4120-6185-7

Printed in Victoria, BC, Canada. Printed on paper with minimum 30% recycled fibre. Trafford's print shop runs on "green energy" from solar, wind and other environmentally-friendly power sources.

Offices in Canada, USA, Ireland and UK

Book sales for North America and international:
Trafford Publishing, 6E–2333 Government St.,
Victoria, BC v8t 4p4 CANADA
phone 250 383 6864 (toll-free 1 888 232 4444)
fax 250 383 6804; email to orders@trafford.com
Book sales in Europe:
Trafford Publishing (uk) Ltd., Enterprise House, Wistaston Road Business Centre,
Wistaston Road, Crewe, Cheshire cw2 7rp UNITED KINGDOM
phone 01270 251 396 (local rate 0845 230 9601)
facsimile 01270 254 983; orders.uk@trafford.com
Order online at:
trafford.com/05-1086

10 9 8 7 6 5 4 3 2

Acknowledgments

This book would not have been possible if it was not for my father. His upbringing contributed to my art of negotiations and business thinking.

Many thanks for the late hours that went into the cover concept and photography by Peter Cherpack - NightfallPhotography.com.

I especially want to thank my wife and daughter for their help, support, and encouragement.

Last, but not least, I want to thank my family and friends who shared their time and ideas.

The Insider's Guide to Saving Money grants discounts for volume ordering of 20 or more copies. For further details, please write to:

The Insider's Guide to Saving Money
Special Purchasing Department
P.O. Box 322
Jamison, PA 18929-0322
WWW.MichaelEllenbogen.com

Contents

Préface

If you want to save money, time, and aggravation, then this is one book you will use repeatedly. Not only will it pay for itself, but the information contained in this book will probably earn you money.

This book will show you ways to purchase consumer products at discounted prices. In most cases, the more you buy and spend on products, the more you will save. My years of experience, and the use of my skills, will help you save money when purchasing cars, homes, appliances, toys, electronics, and just about anything else. You will learn ways to handle customer service issues and receive the respect you deserve as a consumer.

My name is Michael Ellenbogen. Others have told me I am different from most people and that I possess a unique set of skills. They have urged me to go into my own business and charge for my services. I frequently share my ideas with friends and family and they always profit from my advice. I now want to reach out to everyone. Use of this information could eventually improve the way consumers are treated, not to mention what this information can do for you. Remember, the more these skills are used, the more you and your families will benefit. I would like to live in a world where the consumer has rights again, instead of being treated like a second-class citizen. In today's world, companies and businesses put up roadblocks in order to cut costs. This ends up compromising customer service.

This book may be small, but you will gain a wealth of information from it. It will help you today and throughout your lifetime. I used to believe the best book to give someone for a house-warming gift was a how-to-fix-it book for items in and around your home. I now believe this book is much more important to own. This book was written so that everyone can benefit from it, beginning in the teenage years, continuing well into retirement. Keep this book somewhere handy where the whole family can utilize it.

The book is divided into chapters by the topic to be addressed, complete with step-by-step procedures for you to follow. At the end of each chapter, I have also added Helpful Hints / Comments for the topic discussed. It is important to read the entire chapter, including the Helpful Hints / Comments section, to be successful in using these new skills. The final chapter contains additional suggestions that can save you money. There is a glossary in the back to explain words or terms that may be unfamiliar to you. Throughout the book, I often refer to the use of the *Internet*. I realize many people do not have access to a computer or the Internet, but do not let that stop you. Most public libraries have computers with free Internet access. There may even be an Internet café, in your area, where you can relax and order your favorite café latté while surfing the Internet. These cafés charge a small fee for the use of their computers, but you will probably save that money in other ways. The reason I recommend the Internet is that it saves you so much time and gives you access to an enormous amount of information. Tips for using the Internet are available under "Internet Searches" in Chapter 8.

I give many real-life examples throughout the book. You do not need to follow each word to be successful. Most dialogs will be different and will depend on the situation. The information is there to provide direction. You will probably invent many ideas of your own as you go through life. You should role-play, in your mind, the first one or two times you try these techniques. The more you use these skills, and teach others how to use them, the easier it will become.

There is one important message I want you to remember. **The time you spend doing research will pay for itself in the end.** Think of it as being the head of your own company and you are paying yourself to conduct research on the topic, or issues, at hand. The good news is that the money you earn is all yours and you do not even have to share it with Uncle Sam. Best of all, you will walk away with a feeling of satisfaction because you either saved time, money, aggravation, or a combination of the three. I find it very interesting that most people pay whatever the price tag is marked, while other people tend to get great deals. Do you think that is fair? I do not. It would really be nice if we all paid the same amount for the same item. You need to look out for yourself. This book is your opportunity to fight back and stop paying for others. Maybe one day soon we will all be treated equally. You will not have to walk away wondering if you were taken or if you made a good deal.

General Tips:

The following tips should be considered when reading most of the chapters in this book. Definitions and/or more information on words appearing in italics can be found in the glossary section.

> Look for toll-free numbers to call (also referred to as "800" numbers). If you have to call a long distance number, ask the company representative if he/she has a toll-free number you could call back on. (Sometimes you can call an 800 number in a different *department*, such as customer service, and have the representative transfer you to the department you need.) Remember not all toll-free numbers start with area code 800. Some start with 877, 888, 866, and 855.

> Some businesses accept *collect calls*. When calling collect, tell the operator you are a customer calling.

> Always get the name of the employee, or ID number (identification) of the person you are speaking to, no matter what form of communication you are using (face to face, phone, *E-mail*, letter). You never know when that information may be important.

> Never buy a *gray unit* item. (See glossary)

Check with the manufacturer to ensure that an item will be covered under *warranty* if a business is not included on the manufacturers *authorized dealer* list.

I believe credit cards are a very useful tool as long as you can control your spending habits. If you cannot then you should cut them up and throw them away.

To optimize your success in receiving great service, refer to people by name, when conversing in person or on the telephone. The person you are speaking to will be less likely to treat you poorly or hang up on you if that person knows you know his/her name.

Always stop and think about a purchase before you make it. People often jump into things and later have regrets for one reason or another. Many people are *compulsive* shoppers and buy things they do not really need.

Chapter 1

Buying Electronic Equipment, Appliances, Toys, Gym Equipment, etc.

This chapter will probably be the most helpful because these are items most of us purchase throughout the year. The most important thing to remember is: **There is always someone out there willing to make less of a *profit* on a product and make up the difference by selling in volume.** As a consumer, you owe it to yourself not to over-pay for a product. It amazes me how much prices can vary from one business to another. I have actually seen mark-ups of as much as 500% on certain items. Keep in mind not all businesses are trying to take advantage of you. In some cases, the business you are dealing with may not receive the same discount as its *competitors*. Other things that can affect pricing are the neighborhood, the region of the country, a new business versus established businesses, stock availability, time of the month or year and many other factors.

I explain a few different ways to save money when purchasing these products. The information is presented using real-life examples. These techniques can be modified for a wide variety of purchases. Many people do not realize that you can negotiate the ticket prices on many products. These include stereos, washers and dryers, jewelry, home gym equipment, bicycles, furniture, etc. The list goes on and on.

The Internet is probably one of the most powerful tools for helping you obtain the best price, and finding information on new or older items. You can find reliable information at the manufacturers' *Web* sites. Most salespeople do not have a very good understanding of the products they sell. They sometimes give incorrect information or mistakenly mislead you. Remember, most stores have a high employee turnover rate and employees are often shifted from one department to another. (Just think of your own job; we are asked to do more with less in today's world.) It is not the fault of the salespeople. He/she is doing the best they can with the limited resources and training they are given.

When shopping by phone or Internet, you can usually avoid paying sales tax on items that are purchased outside of your home state as long as the business you are dealing with does not have a presence in your state. Many times shipping charges are about the same amount as the tax. By law, you are supposed to pay any sales tax due in your own state. Check your local laws.

You will eventually run into high-pressure salespeople. He/she offers you a great deal at the moment, but they tell you they will not be able to honor that price once you leave. You should reply, "I need to check out one or two other locations on my list before making a commitment. Thanks for the offer. I will get back to you." Do not allow them to pressure you into making the purchase or giving them a deposit. He/she will usually honor the price the next day if you think it over and decide you want to purchase that product after all. Do not be tricked if they tell you it is the last one and someone else might buy it. That is a chance you take, but most likely others can be ordered (unless the item is discontinued). Sometimes it may be a fantastic deal and you may want to say yes right then and there. You should make that decision only if you have done your homework and have a very good idea of the actual *wholesale* cost of the product.

Remember to read the Helpful Hints / Comments section in combination with the examples to gain the most information.

Example 1:   Purchasing a new vacuum cleaner

1. First, identify what features or options you are looking for. If you already have a specific vacuum cleaner in mind, get the model number and skip down to step #3.
    If you are unfamiliar with the features available, check out the various brands to see what they offer and how much they charge. You could visit

a few *retail* stores that carry a large variety. Or you could call them to save time, money on gas, and aggravation. Most manufacturers are willing to mail you literature on products of interest to you. It is also easy to visit a few Web sites to do your comparison-shopping. There are also multiple Web sites where you can get consumer feedback with actual customer comments and product ratings. (Keep in mind, though, anybody can complete those surveys, including people who work for the companies.)

2. Once you determine the vacuum that best fits your needs, jot down the manufacturer's name and model number. Be sure to get the actual manufacturer model number and not the item number associated with that particular store. If you are in the store, look for the model number on the rear or bottom of the product. The serial number usually follows the model number. It is printed on a small label that may be paper, plastic, or aluminum.

3. Locate multiple stores that sell the model you want and keep track of who offers the lowest price. There are three ways to do this. You can visit individual stores and look for that model. You can locate stores in the phone book and call to see if they carry it. Or, in most cases, you can search on the Internet, using the manufacturer's model number, to locate stores that sell that product. Sometimes, searching by model number alone may give you results for products other than the vacuum cleaner you are searching for. If that happens, you will want to use both the model number and manufacturer's name in your search. I have found adding certain words to your search criteria will often return Web sites that offer lower

prices; low, cheap, bargain, best price, discount, sale, etc.

Conduct multiple searches using various Internet search engines (Yahoo, Google, Excite, Lycos etc.) to ensure you are provided with a wide range of companies from which to choose. Keep track of the sites that seem to have the best prices. Write down the price of the item, phone number, and Web site information for each site, in case you want to return to it later.

Call companies with toll-free numbers to verify all applicable costs so that you may accurately compare pricing information. Be sure to include taxes, shipping, and handling charges, etc. Verify that the item comes with all of the components included in your original selection. Sometimes they offer extra hoses, belts, or an *extended warranty*. Sometimes you do not get all of the components. Make certain the product they are offering you is new, in a sealed box. Some businesses offer items that are refurbished, used, or gray units. You do not want to use the pricing for units like these when negotiating pricing on new items.

4. Now take the lowest price you found and negotiate an even better price. Let us say the best price you found was $250.00. Contact one of the businesses offering this price and tell them you have a price offer, from another business, of $205.00 to purchase the same vacuum. The salesperson will either match the price, or tell you the price you quoted is below his/her cost for the product. You should then say, "You're kidding, how can the other business do that?" Wait for his/her response. Then say, "By the way, I'm curious, what does it cost you?" The salesperson

will often tell you what they pay for it. If not, ask them what price he/she would offer if you were to buy it from them.

If that salesperson was able to match the price, call another business and tell them you can get the vacuum for $190.00, and you want to know if they can offer you a better deal. Continue in this fashion until you feel sure you have gotten the best possible price.

Remember the business, to which you are making the offer, is there to make money. They are usually not going to sell you an item that cost them three hundred dollars for a $5.00 to $10.00 profit. (They may if you are buying more than one item at the same time. They may also sometimes be willing to gain you as a new customer.)

5. When you are ready to make the purchase, I recommend you use a credit card that pays you money back for each use. This is another way to save on the purchase. (It also ensures you have the credit card company to use in your defense should you later have a dispute with the business you are buying the vacuum from.)

    Avoid companies with a no return policy. Conduct research on the company you are about to do business with by contacting the Better Business Bureau (BBB) or other organization that perform the same function, just to be safe.

6. If you purchase/order the item from home, ask the business you order from to send you an E-mail or fax to *confirm* the order. Ask them when they plan to ship it, and when you should expect to receive the item.

7. When the vacuum cleaner arrives, be sure to check it out right away. The box should not look as though it has been repacked. Look for signs of previous use. Test the item out to ensure all the features are working. If you have any issues with the item, let the business know immediately. Keep track of the person you spoke with, along with the date and time, and what was said. If everything is OK, hold on to the box for a month or two, just in case you need to send it back, or return it to the store.

8. If you decide to buy from a local business, you will have to pay the taxes, but you will not have to pay shipping and handling charges. Call ahead and ask the manager, or owner, of your local business if they will match the price you received. Tell them you would rather keep the business locally, especially since you have dealt with them in the past. (Some businesses actually take an extra 10% off the difference between their price and the price they are matching, for an even greater discount.)

9. Congratulations!
    These skills and techniques can be used on any item you are considering for purchase. I actually purchased my vacuum cleaner using this approach and saved over $100.00. I even received an extended warranty, extra bags, and hoses.

Most people think you can only haggle over price when buying a car or a home. Remember that many prices are negotiable, especially larger ticket items. I have had people tell me the price is not negotiable, only to accept my offer or lower their price as I was leaving the store or hanging up the phone. You can even make offers on low-priced items and receive discounts. This is especially true if you have seen the same item cheaper somewhere else. Sometimes you can even just say you saw it somewhere else for less. The key is to let them know that you really would like to do business with them.

My next example involves buying an item at your local store. This may not work at some of the small mom and pop stores. The small business cannot compete with the large chain store's discounts. The large business focuses more on volume and receives greater discounts because they buy in bulk. (Conduct your own research before going to the store because many salespeople do not have a very good understanding of the products they sell.)

Example 2:   Purchasing a DVD that sells for $19.95 at your favorite local store.

1.   First, look through the Sunday newspaper. Check out the advertisements and see if another store has that item on sale. If you find the item at a better price, say $14.97, cut out the ad.

2.   You could call a few other businesses at this time, or you could use the Internet to check further for a better price. In most cases, the model number of the item is included in the advertisement. Call the store if you cannot find the model number. Ask for the department manager responsible for DVDs. Tell the manager you are looking at the store's sales flyer and were wondering what the model number is. Some DVDs may be packaged differently, and the cost may not be the same.

3.   Take the newspaper or Internet printout to your favorite store and inform the salesperson you would like to purchase the DVD in that store and you would like him/her to match the price in the ad. If the salesperson says he/she cannot do that, kindly say, "I know you may not have the power to authorize this. I would like to speak with the store manger or owner, please." (You could speak to a department manager but he/she usually does

not have the authority to make these adjustments.) When the manager arrives, tell him/her you are looking for a *price match* because you are a loyal customer, and would rather give them the business than give it to the other store. You do not need to be confrontational, just be firm about your request. Most stores will match the price rather than lose a customer to someone else.

4. These procedures make it easy to do all of your shopping in one place. Remember that you can use these techniques for many items you purchase. This in turn will save you time, money, and aggravation. If you are unable to influence the store manager to match the price of the item, after you have followed the example, you need to refer to the section on Customer Service Issues in Chapter 3. Do not give up.

The next example involves purchasing a sofa. You have seen it in a show room and you have an interest in it. You would like to buy it but the store does not seem reliable, and the price is very high. You ask the salesperson for the manufacturer's name and model number. He gives you the information, you contact other furniture stores, but nobody seems to have it in stock. In fact, most people tell you the model number you have is not a valid number for that manufacturer.

Example 3: Purchasing a leather sofa cheaper, and at a different business location (original price $1,899.00).

1. First, you need to call the business where you originally saw the sofa and ask the salesperson to give you the information again. Tell him you lost the paperwork you had with the information on it. You need to let him know who you are and to describe the sofa you were interested in. After he gives you the information you requested, ask the

salesperson again if he can give you his best price. Tell him/her you are planning to shop around.

2. If you now have the correct model number, skip ahead to #5. If the salesperson gives you the same model number you got at the store, it may mean the place is trying to throw you off so you cannot easily shop around. Only that particular store or chain uses that model number. In order to get the correct manufacturer model number, you will need to return to the business where you first saw the sofa. All furniture that is made out of any type of fabric, leather, etc., has a LAW Label, which has the manufacturer information on it (it is illegal to remove this tag before the item is sold and delivered). You may be able to find model numbers on other furniture items on the back of the item, or inside a drawer. On sofas, it is usually a tag that hangs down from one of the seams, or is stapled on the bottom. Tilt the sofa back and look for the name, address, and model number for the manufacturer. If the salesperson asks why you are doing this, tell them you are looking at the construction and wanted more detail on the manufacturer. You would like to do further research on the manufacturer to ensure they are reputable. Sometimes these stores are tricky and they remove the label. They put on their own internal store number that will probably match the original number they gave you. If you do not see a real manufacturer number, ask the salesperson to show you other furniture pieces made by the same manufacturer. You will usually be able to find at least one item that has the manufacturer name even if you cannot find the correct model number. (Look for a new sofa that may still have the wrapping on it.) At this time, jot down all the dimensions of the sofa and a description of key features. If you now have the correct model

number and manufacturer name, skip ahead to step #5. If you were only able to get the name of the manufacturer, proceed to step #3.

3. Try to call a few businesses that carry that brand and describe the sofa. If they do not seem to know the sofa you are describing, ask them if they can give you the regional sales representative's phone number, or the manufacturer's number. Ask for a toll-free number.

4. Once you have the information, call the manufacturer or the regional sales representative responsible for that store. He/she will know what items that particular store carries in their *inventory*. Let them know you want to purchase a sofa that you saw at (name of the business), along with the (city) and (state). You will need to describe the sofa and its location within the store. The representative should be able to give you the correct model number. Ask the sales representative for the names of other authorized dealers, in your area, that carry that specific model, or can order it. If the person asks why you do not want to deal with the original business, tell them you just would rather not deal with that business and would like to leave it at that.

5. Call some other businesses and see if they have a match on the new model number. (The easiest way to locate other businesses is by checking the yellow pages in the phone book. Find the furniture section and start calling them one by one.) If they do carry the sofa, or can order it, ask them for the complete cost including taxes and delivery charges. If they give you a price of $1,650.00, tell them you received a better offer from another business, but you really would rather not deal with the other business. The salesperson will then ask

you what the other business is willing to sell the sofa for. Tell him the purpose of your call is to get the best price his store is willing to offer. (If you tell him the price he needs to beat first, you may only get a small discount.) The salesperson may respond with a better offer. In any case, you can then tell the salesperson the other business was going to sell the item to you for $311.01 - $411.01 below the price that was just given to you (you can select any dollar amount, I like to end mine with one to three cents). *This number is not real. It should be lower than you think the store pays for the sofa, but not so low it is completely unrealistic. At this point you are trying to find out what the wholesale price is.* Tell the salesperson you want his best price. He may come back and say the price you quoted is below the cost that his company pays for the sofa. Act surprised and say, "You're kidding. I know the price was correct because I verified the price with the business." How can the other business offer it so low and you can't." Wait for his/her response. Then say, "By the way, I'm curious, what does it cost you?" The salesperson will usually tell you what the store pays for the item. At that point ask them, "How much would you charge me if I were to do business with you?" Once you have a price quote, thank the person and tell them you will recheck with the other business in case they made a mistake.

If the salesperson says he can sell you the sofa for $1,238.99, it means you did not reach the wholesale price. You should call a few more businesses and go through the same process, but this time lower the amount you quote them by $100.00 - $200.00.

6. Once you have determined the wholesale price, it is fair to pay $50.00 to $150.00 over that amount.

(The more items you buy from that store, the less they need to make on each item.) Call or visit the store where you wish to purchase the sofa. Speak to the owner or store manager and tell them you have received a price of ___ for the sofa at another business ($50.00 - $150.00 over whatever you determined the wholesale price to be). Tell them you would like to purchase the item from them, if they will match the price. (Sometimes you may need to negotiate a little if you quote too low a price.) If they are not willing to do that, contact another business and make them the same offer. You will be able to negotiate a great deal.

All this takes a little effort and may become discouraging at times. Then you finally seal the deal and you saved $500.00 - $900.00. That moment makes it all worthwhile.

You will get better and better at this each time you do it. It may seem tough at first, but your progress will be its own reward. Where else can you make that kind of money for one or two hour's work? Do not feel badly about deceiving them about the price. Most businesses are not playing fairly either. They charge based on what you are willing to pay.

Helpful Hints / Comments:

If you do not have access to the Internet, visit your local library or bookstore. Check out reference books and magazines related to your topic. Look for items that have current dates to ensure you are getting accurate information.

Always inspect boxes received by mail as soon as they arrive. If a box appears to be badly damaged or you notice exposed contents, do not open it. Refuse the shipment and have it sent back. Call the business and let them know what happened. This will save you a lot of aggravation. If you sign for the item and find it is damaged, call and notify the business that shipped it to you, as well as the company that delivered it.

Check to see if the manufacturer or business is offering customer rebates for any of the items you are purchasing. Many times you will find customer rebate slips near the customer service desk, or at the front of the store near the registers. Always ask for a duplicate receipt to use for the rebate. Hold on to your original receipt because most stores will not accept copies for returns or a price match.

Be wary of stores that offer 30-day satisfaction *guarantees* for furniture, mattresses, etc. The manufacturers usually do not take these products back after they are returned to the store. You may be buying a product that was already used by somebody else. Check all items for signs of use before purchasing.

Be sure to save your receipt. You may need it in the future.

Furniture prices vary for many different businesses. Be careful because other manufacturers may make copies of some of the best selling styles. You cannot always tell the quality by the price. Always compare the manufacturer name and model number. Most of the time, the construction of the copy is cheaply made, even though it looks good on the outside.

Sometimes businesses purposely change the model number by one digit to throw you off when comparing prices. Some manufacturers actually make the identical product for certain businesses, or store chains, and they have a slightly different model number. (This protects the seller. They do not have to match prices on the product because they are the only one that carries that specific model number.)

Always add up all costs for receiving a product when comparing pricing. (Actual product cost, surcharge if order below minimum dollar amount, handling fees, shipping fees and non-member fees.)

Be careful when you are trying to save money. Sometimes saving money can cost you more in the long run. Here is an example. A person went out and bought a one-sided mattress but saved a lot of money. One-sided mattresses cannot be flipped over. After a while, most mattresses need to be flipped because of the impressions that occur. Always look at things long term. On the other hand, if you knew you would have to replace the mattress in a year or two, the one-sided mattress could be the best buy at the time. For example, you bought a twin sized bed because you had no room in your present house, and you knew you were planning to move in a year or two and would need a larger one. Then you would save money by buying the less expensive mattress for that short period of need.

Always ask for the cheapest delivery option. It usually takes four or five days longer. In some cases, you will still receive the item in the same timeframe even though you chose the cheaper rate.

Do not pay for added insurance against damage or theft if you are the receiver of a shipment. Most state laws hold the carrier or sender responsible for all issues until the package is delivered. Check with your state laws. If paying by credit card, you might be automatically insured under the credit card company's policy. This does not apply to the United States Postal Service.

Do not buy a used item just because it is inexpensive. Check it out thoroughly to avoid dealing with the aggravation that could arise if something goes wrong.

Chapter 1

Do not always think you are safe because you are buying a recognized brand name product. Many manufacturers sell to a wide range of retailers. Some of their products may be of poor quality, while others may be the best in their category. Some businesses are aware of this, while others are not. The manufacturers do this in order to attract customers of different income levels. Some rely on their past reputation and name recognition to sell products today, even though they may no longer sell the best quality products.

Many people feel it is not worth their time to save money on a low priced item, but small savings can add up over time. Every time you save $10.00, it is equivalent to your employer paying you $12.50 or more before taxes. If you still feel you do not have time to research ways to save, ask your children to do the research. Offer to split the savings with them if he/she can find you a better deal than what you were planning to spend for the product. This will benefit them in two ways. It will teach them at an early age the value of being patient and a smart shopper, and he/she will earn money at the same time.

Chapter 2

Vehicles and Other Expensive Items

When it comes to buying or leasing a new vehicle, most people really do not like dealing with the aggravation. This should be a happy time. In most cases, the problem is the pressure of dealing with the sales folks, and the questions you are left with when the deal is completed. Did I pay too much? Was the deal as good as I thought it was? Many people pay more than they should and, in some cases, they actually pay the *sticker price*. I have even heard of people paying hundreds or thousands of dollars over sticker price for a new car model that was in high demand. The sad part is that when the novelty wears off, the car's value will drop substantially. In fact, if the car were totaled in an accident the day it was purchased, the insurance company would only pay you sticker price, if you were lucky.

Purchasing

I will show you how to turn purchasing a car into a more pleasant experience. You will not feel like you were taken by the salesperson. In fact, you could save from $200.00 to $5,000.00 depending on the vehicle. The best time to get a good price when you buy a vehicle is at the end of the month. To increase your chances of getting the best deal, it helps if it is raining, snowing, or very hot outside. It also helps if the dealer has many vehicles like the one you want in stock, if you are buying last year's model, or if it is the slow season for the business (February tends to be the slowest month, followed by September). A combination of these factors is even better. The best you could hope for is to go to the dealership on a snowy day in late February. They have the car you want on the lot, just came out with the new model, and you are using your new skills. I know we cannot always time the purchase of a new car because our vehicles break down unexpectedly. It may sometimes be cheaper to rent a car for a week or two if it is near the end of the month.

Buying a vehicle is a big decision but too many people do not give it much thought. If this were a house, you would do a great deal of research and thinking about it before making a decision. This is probably the second most expensive thing that people buy. The following car buying information may seem a bit overwhelming. I provide detailed information to help you in dealing with the professional hagglers. A list highlighting the nineteen important steps can be found on page 38.

The toughest part of buying a vehicle is determining which vehicle to buy. Below are just some of the decisions you will need to make when choosing a new car.

- Who, besides me, will be using the vehicle?
- How concerned am I with fuel efficiency?
- Do I want a car that has a very good reliability history?
- Do I have good credit and will I qualify for a low interest loan? What is my credit score? (also known as *FICO Score*)
- How much can I afford to pay each month for the loan?
- Am I concerned with safety crash test results and safety devices?
- How much will insurance cost?
- Do I need a front, rear, or all wheel drive vehicle?
- How much can I get for my present vehicle?
- Does it matter if it is American, or foreign made?
- Do I need a compact, midsize, full-size, sport, or luxury vehicle?
- Do I want a car, van, pickup truck, or utility vehicle?
- If I buy an expensive car, will I worry about where I park it all the time?
- How much do I have for a down payment?
    Try to put at least 20% down. This will keep your monthly payments lower. Do not take out a loan for more than four years in an effort to lower your payments. You will still have loan payments at the time the warranty expires, and you may

need the money for vehicle maintenance. If you have to sell the car before the loan is paid, you may owe more for the vehicle than it is worth.

So where do you start, you ask? Once you answer the preceding questions, you should have some idea of what you want, and what you are willing to spend. I like to keep all of my options open and look at all manufacturers to see what is available. This can be accomplished a few different ways. You can drive to each showroom. You can call each dealer and request that literature be sent to you. (In either case just pick up your local phone book and look in the section labeled Automobile Dealers - New Cars.) Or, if you have access to a computer, the use of the Internet is probably the best option. You can easily visit every manufacturer's Web site from the comfort of your home, whenever you want. You do not need to see salespeople or get any misleading information. The facts are all at your fingertips. To get to the Web sites, in most cases, all you need to do is type the name of the company on the address/location bar, followed by ".com/". You could also perform a search on the manufacturer's name. Once you identify what vehicles you like, you should conduct research on each one to ensure that it is the type of vehicle you want.

There are many Web sites where you can get information about the vehicles you are considering. You will need to know the year, make, model, and the trim or style (DL, DX, GT, GS, LS, LX, etc.) of the vehicle. The amount of information you can retrieve is amazing. You can see lenders, bank rates, pricing, vehicle buying services, safety, feedback from other consumers, independent road tests and reviews, and all the options that are available for that vehicle. My favorite sites allow you to compare various manufacturers' vehicles and features side by side. They are included in the Helpful hints/Comments section at the end of this chapter. I do not specify my favorites as other sites may work better for you. (I would caution you on the integrity of the information you find. I have uncovered a few mistakes in the past.)

Chapter 2

By now you should have narrowed down your selection. Visit your local dealers to look at the vehicles and test drive them. If you are still interested in that model after you drive it, ask the dealer for his/her opinion of the vehicle. Get the complete list of options and packages that are available. Do not spend time discussing price at this time. Just tell the dealer you have narrowed down your selection between this car and that of another manufacturer. Tell him/her you are looking to get the best price and will be back in touch.

Once you have decided which vehicle to purchase, you are ready to conduct your research, or pay someone else to do it. Many services out there charge a fee to provide all you need to know about the vehicle. The information ranges from rebates offered, incentives, warranties, hold back programs, advertisement fees, safety, reliability, dealer's invoice, to how to get the best deal on a vehicle, etc. (Well you know you don't need the part on how to get the best deal because you already have the best book on that topic.) These services usually run anywhere from ten to thirty-five dollars per vehicle. You could also obtain books in the library, bookstores, or information from consumer or automobile magazines. These sources are usually not as detailed and are limited on the information they give you. Incentives and rebates can change anytime, and these resources may not be up to date.

You will need to use the Internet to conduct the rest of your research. Go back to the manufacturers' Web sites for the vehicle you selected. View all of the options that are available and determine if you want to add or eliminate options or packages. New vehicles today often come equipped with many standard features. There may be just a few extra options to select from. Once you know which options you want, you can begin to search out the best price. Many Web sites provide free vehicle pricing information. Check out the Web sites and determine which ones work best for you. I have provided some in the "Helpful hints" section of this chapter. I like to visit at least three sites to ensure the accuracy of the information retrieved.

You need to fill in information about the vehicle, such as the make, model, and year. Then you need to select the options you want on your vehicle. The Web page may request information on the region, state, or zip code you live in. This information is necessary to provide an accurate price for your local area. Some sites will provide a total price, which includes all of the options. Other sites will list the price of the base model, destination charges, and the cost of options, separately. You need to add the price of the options to the base price, plus destination charge, to determine the total price. Most sites have two columns; one is the *dealer invoice* price, or dealer's cost, and the other is the retail, or sticker price, also known as the Manufacturers Suggested Retail Price (MSRP). The price you are most concerned with is the dealer's invoice price, or dealer's cost, because that is what the dealer pays for the vehicle. He/she might actually pay less than that price after the car is sold. It depends on how much they receive at the end of the month, in kickbacks, from the manufacturer. The retail price is what the dealer would like you to pay.

You should now compare pricing at three different sites. They should be about the same, give or take fifteen dollars. Most Web sites do not include advertising costs, which are often added to the invoice price at the dealership. Many dealers will insist you pay this fee. I keep this in the back of my mind, but I do not include it in my offers. There are dealers who are willing to let those charges go. I tell them that is the price of doing business and those expenses can be deducted on the company's tax return. (High volume dealers are more likely not to charge for advertising. Because they sell many vehicles monthly, they receive additional funding from the car manufacturer for reaching set goals.) Advertisement fees run from $200.00 to $500.00.

I like to print out all the information, but you could also write it down on a sheet of paper. If you find any major discrepancies between the Web sites you selected, try another Web site. I like to feel comfortable and have three matching sites, but you are probably okay with two. You will use this information to negotiate with the dealership, so it is important to be accurate.

Most of the sites tell you the date the information is based on. Now that you have done your homework, you are armed with most of the information you need to know.

You need to decide if you want a warranty plan. If you do, what *deductible* do you want $0.0, $25.00, $50.00, or $100.00. How many years and miles do you need coverage for? Call a dealer to see what is available from the manufacturer and the cost. Most warranties range from about $600.00, to about $2,700.00 in price. It depends on what options you choose.

Create a complete list containing all of the information about the car. Make this list easy to read because you will keep it in front of you as you are negotiating with the dealer. You should be prepared to tell the dealer what vehicle you want along with what packages and options. The more information you have on the vehicle, the easier it will be to explain to them how you arrived at that price. This will make it easier to bargain for the best possible price. See figure A, on page 26, for an example.

Go back to the manufacturer's Web sites and look for the sections that show the dealer location. Select dealers up to a two hundred-fifty mile radius from your home. If you live in a rural area then you may look a little farther out. Make a list of the dealerships including the name, address, fax number, and phone number (toll-free numbers preferred).

For the purpose of this example, let us say the vehicle you researched cost $18,500.00 (dealer's invoice price), including all of the options you selected, and the destination charge. Do not include the advertising cost, but keep it in the back of your mind. As you speak to dealers, or when they fax offers, you will be able to determine the advertising cost, if any. Just tell them you do not pay those charges. I will assume you are going to choose a 7 year, 100,000 mile warranty with a $0 deductible that provides *bumper-to-bumper* coverage.

Example 1:   Wish to purchase a new vehicle with a 7 year, 100,000-mile warranty with a $0 deductible.

1. The first thing you need to do is to be prepared with the list you wrote earlier, including the vehicle information and options. Different vehicles will have different option codes. See figure A for an example of my list.

Figure A

(Year) (Make name) (Model name) (What colors am I willing to buy?)

(Code) (List of extra options that are not standard on the base model)
TC   Traction control
A3   ABS brakes
MUD   Mudguards
P1   This is the options package which includes air conditioning, premium stereo w/ CD, upgraded wheels.

Dealer Invoice price (Including options I selected)	$18,500.00	MSRP $21,328.00
Your offer over Invoice	$ 200.00	
Estimated extended warranty for 7 years, 100,000 miles with $0.0.deductible	$ 900.00	
Total price	**$19,600.00**	

2. Now you are ready to make the first call, so get your list of phone numbers ready. You are probably wondering, what about my old vehicle? I will get to that later but do not tell the salesperson you have a trade-in at this point. If they ask, just say you plan to keep your present vehicle. When you start making the calls, it is important to act and feel confident about what you are saying. Think of it as playing a role in a movie and you are the star. Well maybe not a star, but you will feel like one after you make your deal. Start by calling the toll-free numbers of dealers that are farthest away from your location. (Dealers that are

far away tend to give you better deals. Dealers look at you as a possible new customer. They know you are far away and they want to attract you, so they give you a good deal.) Also, at this time you are just trying to determine the rock bottom price you will be able to purchase the car for. You probably will not end up buying from the dealership that is farthest away. You need to have a firm offer to use when you speak with the dealer that is most convenient for you.

Let us get started and call the first number. When the dealership answers the phone, ask for the sales manager of the department that sells the make of vehicle you are looking to buy. Once you have the manager on the phone, skip to paragraph #3. (If you did not call an 800 number ask the receptionist if the company has an 800 number.) Then ask the receptionist to transfer you to the manager's *voicemail.* Leave the following message. "Hi my name is ____; I'm calling you because I would like to purchase a vehicle from you. I already have a fairly good price, but I know I could do much better. Since the price is very low and does not leave much room for profit, I came to you directly. I am a very good negotiator and I know I can get a better deal from you. I am willing to come to your location to pick up the car. I am looking to buy a (year, make, model) vehicle. Please call me back so we can go over the options and make a deal. (Leave your area code and phone number.) Thanks in advance and have a nice day."

If the manager does not have voicemail, leave a message with the receptionist. Ask the manager to call you back as you would like to speak to him personally about buying a vehicle. Give the receptionist the make, model, and year of the vehicle you are interested in and leave your phone number, including area code. Once you have the manager on the phone, proceed to paragraph #3.

3. "Hi my name is ___, I am calling you because I want to buy a (year, make, model) vehicle. I already have a fairly good price but I know could do better. I was always a very good negotiator and I always do my homework." He/she may tell you at this time that they do not haggle on the price. I would say, "It's up to you. I could either continue or take my business elsewhere." If there is still no interest, just start over with another dealer. Otherwise, continue where you left off. "I came to you directly because there is not much room for profit in the deal. I did not know if you wanted me to deal with you directly or use a salesperson, since you are not going to make much profit on this sale. I just want to let you know where I am coming from. The last few cars I purchased were bought from $50.00 to $200.00 over invoice. As you can see I have done pretty well for myself." Whatever you do, do not let the salesperson know what your lowest price is. He may ask, "Well, what price do I need to beat?" You respond by saying, "I'm not going to tell you that. I just want you to give me your best possible price so you and I can do business. You will not only gain me as a customer but I'll send my friends to you if you offer them the same good deals." Tell him you are looking for a total package deal. Give him all the information about the vehicle, options, and warranty, but no price figures from your sheet. Tell him the other place that gave you the offer is passing the warranty on to you at cost. The other dealership is just charging you for the vehicle and options. Tell him to work up his best deal and get back to you with one price for everything. Tell him he is going to have to work extra hard on this

deal, but it will be worth it to gain you as a customer. He may tell you the car is not available because he does not have it, or he may not have the color that you are requesting. Tell him you are willing to wait in order to get a good deal, or you may even be willing to take the color he has on the lot. He may ask you how soon you want the car. Tell him if the numbers look good, you can be there in a few days. Ask him to subtract all incentives, cash back, and rebates when he is working out the numbers. (These are probing questions. Keep track of any incentives or rebates he mentions. Ask him when they expire, if they have rebates or incentives.) If the manager says there are none say, "I thought so but was just checking to see if anything changed in the past few days." Tell the manager to work his magic and get back to you. Ask the manager when you can expect a return call.

Some people just write down the vehicle information and options and fax it to the dealership. (See figure B for example on page 31) Make them aware that you did your homework and are a good negotiator. You do this by breaking down each option and show the Dealers invoice price and the retail price. If you are aware of any incentives or rebates, list them on the sheet. If not, write at the bottom of the sheet that you are faxing, "Please provide me with your best price. I am aware of your dealer holdback program, cash back, incentives and rebates that are being offered. Your final price offer should include those discounts. Thank you for your time and I look forward to doing business with you." You can request them to call you with the *bottom line* price, or he/she can fax it back to you. Make sure the dealer has a couple of ways to get in touch with you, along with your name and phone number. It always helps if you can personally send it to someone's attention at the dealership. In order to do this, you will need to call the dealership and ask for the names of the following positions- fleet manager, sales manager, and Internet sales manager for your make vehicle. Fleet mangers usually do not get paid *commissions* so they are usually willing to give you a better deal. Keep in mind that not all dealers have all three positions or three separate people in those positions. It could be the same person just wearing different hats. You may even try the same location again, if you got a good price back, by faxing to one of the other positions. Try to stay away from weekends and after 3 PM daily because they tend to be much busier during those periods. Faxing is OK if you do not feel comfortable talking to a salesperson. I personally do not like this method because I get more information by using probing questions. I sometimes combine the two. I will fax first and then follow-up with a phone call.

You can also obtain quotes from Internet car dealerships. If you do not like to haggle, or just do not feel comfortable doing that, then this is the perfect solution for you. There are many sites where you can enter the car, and options you are looking for, and they will respond with a price within 24-48 hours. I supplied you with some of those sites also. The price is usually not bad. It is better than just going to buy a car at a dealership and paying almost the MSRP. The problem with these referral places is that they have set discounts and are usually not willing to go much lower. Sometimes they actually come back with some surprisingly low numbers. I have heard of deals for $200.00 over invoice. It is usually more around $500.00 over invoice. They are only good for new car buying and you are still entitled to any of the rebate programs. Most of these places will handle your trade, and some are actually willing to deliver the car to your door. That is a lot better than dealing with any showroom salesperson.

Figure B

To: Sales Managers Name
From: Your Name
My Fax Number is _____
My Phone Number is _____

I'm looking to purchase the vehicle below with the following options.

(Year) (Make name) (Model name) (What colors I am willing to buy?)

Code	List of all extra options that are not standard in the base model
TC	Traction control
A3	ABS brakes
MUD	Mudguards
P1	This is the options package that includes air conditioning, premium stereo w/ CD, upgraded wheels.

Dealer Invoice price (includes all options added in & Destination Charge.)

Dealers Invoice   **$18,500.00**   MSRP $21,328.00

I would also like you to include, in your total price, the following extended warranty for 7 years, 100,000 miles with $0.0 deductible. I'm looking for you to pass along the extended warranty to me at your cost.

Please provide me with your best price; I am aware of your dealer holdback program, cash back, incentives and rebates that are being offered. Your final offer should include those discounts. Please fax the information back, or feel free to contact me in person should you have any questions.

Thank you for your time. I look forward to doing business with you now and in the future.

4. If you do not hear back from anyone by the time specified, call them back. (You are not a very high priority because they will not make a lot of money on your deal.) They may have a salesperson call you back to finalize the numbers. If a salesperson calls you back, go over the items in paragraph #3. It will let him know the type of person you are. Unless of course he is just calling to give you a price, then move on to the next paragraph.

5. When he finally gives you the number, assuming it is higher than the researched price of $19,600.00, say, "That's the best you can do?" (Let us say he offers you 19,975.00.) "You are way off; you need to do a lot better than that." The salesperson will probably ask what the dollar amount is that he/she needs to beat to get your business. Tell them, "If I give you the bottom line, you will only beat it by a few dollars, and I'm looking for a bigger savings." The salesperson will probably come down to $19,799.00. I would say at this point, "You are still off a couple hundred dollars," and pause. The salesperson may say that's a great deal and I cannot match that. You should say, "I would really like to do business with you so I'm going to tell you what the other dealer offered me." At this point, you tell the person $19,600.00 and pause. The person may ask the breakdown of the cost. Just tell them the paper you have has the total price only, with all options and warranty listed and included, except for tax. At this point the person may have to call you back. If he matches your price or beats it, go to paragraph #8.

The person may say the price is cheaper than what he pays for the vehicle. Just say, "You're kidding." Maybe the other dealer made a mistake in the figures. If he cannot match or beat the price, ask him, "Well what is the invoice price for the vehicle and warranty cost to you?" (If he tells you, you now have the information you need to continue.) If this dealer has the car on the lot that you want, I would ask him for his best price again because you liked working with him and may still consider doing business with him if the other place made a mistake. If he sticks with the same price, I would say, "Come on you could do better."

6. At this point, I would start the process with another dealer that is still located far away from you. Return to paragraph #3 and start again. I do this to confirm information from other dealers in case one or two of the dealers just did not want to do business due to the minimal profit margin. If you feel comfortable doing this I actually place my calls, in one sitting, to 3 or 4 dealers. You just need to keep close track of your conversations and where you left off.

7. I will assume the dealer has made an offer to sell you the vehicle for $19,550.00. This means you are closer and probably have a good deal at this time, but I would recommend you try to do even better. I would now take the $19,550.00 and subtract $200.00. This now brings your new rock bottom price to **$19,350.00**. Use this new lowest price and start again at paragraph #3, calling dealerships located closer and closer to home. Continue this process over and over until you have determined that the dealer is only making $50.00 to $200.00 on your sale. When you reach the best price, go on to paragraph #9.

8. You should be proud of yourself. You probably spent 3 or 4 hours in total from the comfort of your home and did not have to put up with the pressure that most salespersons use. This time, you were in control, not them. I bet it felt good. You only have a few more steps to complete.

9. You have to make a few more decisions. What are you going to do with your existing vehicle? *No vehicle, go to paragraph 10.* The first thing you need to do is find out the value of the vehicle in terms of the wholesale and retail price. You first need to know the make, model, year, miles, condition of the vehicle inside and out, and what major options are installed. Once you have this information, there are free sites on the Internet to check used car prices. You can also go to your local library, bookstore, read a newspaper or stop by a dealer. The first thing you should do is wash and wax the vehicle. There are waxes available that have colors that match the color and shade of the car. These waxes are good for hiding minor scratches. Take care of any minor visible issues that stand out (Stain on paint, spot on seat, burned bulb, car smells like cigarettes, etc.) Vacuum the inside and detail the car as well as you can. When a dealer looks at your vehicle, he/she will scrutinize every little chip and mark so that they can offer you a lower price. Tell them the car really needs a good cleaning and waxing. You just tried to make it presentable a few weeks ago. Have a few dealers give you a bid. When they make you an offer, act surprised and say, "I'm sure I have been told it was worth at least $1,200.00 more than that." If you are the original owner or have all of the maintenance records let them know because that usually adds value. Keep in mind that a dealer will usually give you the vehicle's wholesale price. After he gives you the

price again say, "I think you could do better than that." Before leaving, ask the person how long he/she will hold that offer for you. Other sources can provide you with both the wholesale and retail price. These prices change every month. Now you need to decide if you are going to sell the car yourself or trade it in when you buy the new car.

10. The last decision you need to make is where you would like to have your vehicle serviced once you buy it. If you already have the same make vehicle, you probably want to use the same dealership, unless of course you are not happy with the service. At this point you will call the dealership, where you would like to purchase your new car, to see if they will beat or match the price. The thing to keep in mind is that not all dealers will give you the same discount. It is even possible that the dealership you choose will be able to offer you an even better deal.

11. When the dealership answers the phone, ask for the sales manager for the department that sells the make of vehicle you are looking to buy. When you have the manager on the phone say, "Hi my name is ___, I am calling you because I have been shopping around for a (year, make, model) vehicle. I have been offered some great prices. I would rather deal with you because you are near my home." (If you presently bring your car to them for service, let them know that.) "The reason I got such a good price is because I am a negotiator and do my homework very well. I came to you directly because there is not much room for profit in this deal. I did not know if you wanted me to deal with you directly or use a salesperson, since you are not going to make much profit on this sale.

Tell him you are looking for a total package deal. Give him all the information about the vehicle, options, and complete warranty details. Tell him the other place that made you the offer is passing the warranty on to you at cost. The other dealership is just charging you for the vehicle and options. Tell him to work up his best deal and get back to you with one price for all. Ask the manager to subtract all incentives, cash back, and rebates when he is working out the numbers. If the manager says there are none, say I thought so, but was just checking to see if anything changed in the past few days. Tell the manager to work his magic and get back to you. If he asks you what the price is that he needs to beat, tell him I usually do not pass this information on, but I do like you and want to finalize the deal as soon as possible. Tell him the lowest price you have been offered. Then tell him you would like him to beat it, not just match it. Tell him you do not just want him to beat it by a few dollars. Ask the manager when you can expect a return call. Tell him everything he wants to know except about any trade. (When you need the car, if a loan is needed, the colors you want, etc.)

12. When he calls back, he will say either he can do it or he cannot. He could be testing you out. Tell him a second dealer has also verified the price so you know the numbers are valid. Tell them he should be able to give you the same deal. If it looks like they do not want to match or beat the price say, "I could just buy the vehicle at the other place and bring it to you for service, but that's not what I want to do." If you already do business with this dealer, I would tell the manager you want to talk to his manager or the owner. Tell him you cannot believe that he is turning away your

business after you have been a loyal customer. That usually works. If the person does not change their mind, then you do not have many options. They may be willing to make the deal for another $50.00 to $100.00. I would ask what it would take to finalize the deal now. If that does not work, take the best deal that you found from the closest dealer and transfer the car to whatever dealership you want to use for service. All warranty issues will be covered the same no matter where you take the vehicle, as long as they are an authorized dealer.

13. No matter where you end up buying the vehicle, do not tell the dealership about the trade. Wait until they give you the complete price. At this point I would tell the salesperson that we have a deal and it was a pleasure doing business. Now tell him you were originally thinking of selling the vehicle on your own but are having second thoughts. He will be able to give you a rough idea of what he can give you but he will need to see the vehicle. Remember that he will only pay you the wholesale price. You already should have some quotes from other dealers. He should be fairly close to the average of all of your other quotes. It is up to you at this point if you trade it in to this dealer or one that may have offered you even more. Or you could sell the car on your own. That may not be easy unless the car is in great condition and it is a popular make and model. There are other risks if you sell it yourself (safety, change in market price, not finding a buyer, added cost for insurance and advertising). You will lose about $700.00 to $2,500.00 if you trade it in, but you do not have any aggravation. It is up to you.

The previous car buying information may seem a bit overwhelming but I just wanted to give you the complete picture on how you should handle the situation. Remember you are dealing with professional hagglers. The bottom line is to remember the following nineteen simple steps.

1. What is your present vehicle worth if you are trading it in?
2. How much can you afford to spend?
3. If you need a loan, how is your credit rating?
4. Check for the best loan rate from banks, credit unions or the Internet sites.
5. What type of vehicle do you want and need?
6. Research vehicles and narrow down your selection.
7. Test drive vehicles and determine one or two you would be happy with.
8. Determine the dealer's invoice price, rebates, and dealer incentives, to determine the best price.
9. How much is an extended warranty on the Internet, if you want one.
10. Go and make your offer. Continue to experiment with pricing at various dealerships to obtain the best price.
11. Once the dealer accepts the offer, let them know about your trade.
12. Decide how to obtain the best return for your present car, by trading it in or selling it privately.
13. If you need a loan let them know you will need a day or two to get your approvals.
14. Take the best loan rate from dealer, bank, credit union, or from the Internet.
15. Call your insurance company and notify them about the changes.
16. Only if the loan is approved, take the car.
17. If you are one of those people that want to pay cash for the new vehicle, check into any financing incentives that may be offered. You may do better to leave your money invested if they offer you 1 or 2% financing. (Sometimes the dealer is paid for loans that he sells, which in turn could be passed on to you as a discount toward the vehicle

purchase. The incentive compensation can range from $50.00 - $500.00.)

18. Inspect the car before leaving the dealer's lot for scratches, dents, etc.
19. Have the dealer make a list of any issues and state when he will resolve them.

Leasing

I have never leased a vehicle myself but I have received requests to include some information on this topic. When you lease a vehicle the dealer is actually selling the car to a finance company or bank (the "Lessor") which in turn charges you (the "Lessee") for the use of the vehicle for a set period of time, usually 3 to 4 years. By the time the lease agreement ends, you have paid for the estimated depreciation of the vehicle plus interest and other fees. You must now return the vehicle to the finance company, or you may have the option to purchase it from them at the pre-determined fixed price. A vehicle depreciates the most in the first 2 years. This explains why your monthly payments are lower when you lease a vehicle for a longer period of time. You are responsible for all maintenance costs during the lease period (brakes, oil changes, tires, plus any other necessary repairs).

Some advantages to leasing a vehicle.
- Lower monthly payments.
- If you plan to change cars every two or three years, leasing may be a better option.
- Sometimes the manufacturer offers some very tempting deals.
- You pay for the amount of time you use the vehicle, not the whole car.
- To obtain use of an expensive car that you would not be able to afford otherwise.
- Moving from one lease to another may be convenient.
- You have a new car every few years.

- You can put the money you save up front toward something that may appreciate in value, such as stock, real estate, etc.

Below are some disadvantages to leasing a vehicle.

- Lease payments do not always include sales tax. Tax advantages or disadvantages depend on the state. Some states tax just the depreciation; others tax just the monthly payment via a "use" tax.
- Terminating a lease early may not be possible, or can be difficult to accomplish. You may be responsible to pay thousands of dollars to buy out the remaining time.
- Finance charges are being paid on the residual and depreciation.
- Lease payments are not always that much lower than purchasing a vehicle, especially on leases over 4 years in length.
- There can be hidden charges, such as excess mileage or usage charges, wear and tear charges, disposition fees (cost for tune-up, final maintenance and cleaning), and early termination fees.
- You usually need to have a good credit rating.
- Insurance can be more expensive because the bank, or finance company, often requires higher coverage limits.
- If you drive more than 15,000 miles per year, your monthly payment will be much higher.
- You make never-ending payments for the use of a vehicle.
- The finance company benefits from the equity as it builds, not you.
- You must return the vehicle to the dealership exactly as it was purchased. You are not able to make any modifications, or personalize it.
- If the car is stolen, or totaled, your insurance may only pay you the market value of the vehicle. This may be less than the amount you owe on your lease agreement. (*GAP insurance* covers this.)

- You must make a vehicle acquisition decision at the end of the lease agreement no matter what the economy is like at the time. You cannot time the market to your advantage.
- The individual numbers used to determine your lease payment may be good, but are you really getting that price in the end? It is difficult to determine if the final lease payment figure is truly a reflection of the agreed upon vehicle price.
- Many dealerships may require that you obtain a new license plate and registration with each new lease term.

The chart on page 42 will help you better understand how expensive leasing can be. For the sake of simplicity, the figures do not include additional costs, such as interest, security deposits, maintenance fees, or service fees other than the actual cost of the vehicle. If these figures were included, the cost of the vehicle would be much higher on the lease. Let us assume you lease a vehicle that has an MSRP of $24,000.00 and your lease term is for 36 months. You plan to drive 12,000 miles per year and the residual value is 45%, which makes this vehicle a bad choice due to its fast depreciation. This vehicle will have a residual value of $10,800.00 at the end of the lease term. That is also what your "buy out" figure would be. (Residual value is usually stated as a percentage of the MSRP. For example, if you lease a vehicle that cost $20,000.00, for 36 months, and its residual is 50%, the car will only be worth $10,000.00 after 3 years.)

As the chart illustrates, you lose 30% ($7,200) in depreciation the first year and the vehicle costs 60 cents per mile to operate. In the third year you lose only 8% ($1,920) and the cost per mile is 16 cents. The first few years are the most expensive.

Now let us make a few more assumptions in reference to the chart. You have a $1,000.00 down payment and are considering either a lease or purchase for 4 years. Both carry an 8% interest rate. (The insurance rate is usually higher on a leased vehicle. I do not include tax, but tax is often higher for the leased vehicle.) The lease monthly payments will be $369.84 and you will spend a total of $18,752.21 over the 48-month term. This includes your $1,000.00 down payment. (You may even have to pay additional wear and tear charges and/or extra mileage charges.)

On the other hand, if you purchase the vehicle your monthly finance payment will be $561.50 and you will spend $26,951.87 over the 48-month period. This also includes your $1,000.00 down payment.

The biggest advantage in the purchase is that you now own the vehicle, with a market value of $9,360 (it is still worth 39% of the purchase price). You have a vehicle that can be used for a few more years. Just two more years of use will contribute to a major savings. The cost per mile is now only .12 cents. Or you can choose to sell it or trade it in on a new car. On the other hand, the leased vehicle must be returned. It leaves you with zero equity.

Year	Annual Depreciation (percent)	Cumulative Annual Depreciation	Annual Residual Value	Annual Depreciation (dollars)	Annual Cost Per Mile
BUY	0	0	24,000	New Vehicle	0
1	30	30	16,800	7,200	.60
2	17	47	12,720	4,080	.34
3	8	55	10,800	1,920	.16
4	6	61	9,360	1,440	.12
5	5	66	8,160	1,200	.10
6	5	71	6,960	1,200	.10
7	4	75	6,000	960	.08
8	4	79	5,040	960	.08
9	3.5	82.5	4,200	840	.07
10	3.5	86	3,360	840	.07
11	3	89	2,640	720	.06
12	3	92	1,920	720	.06
13	2.5	94.5	1,320	600	.05
14	2.5	97	720	600	.05
15	1.5	98.5	360	360	.03
16	1	99.5	120	240	.02
17	.5	100	0	120	.01

If you are concerned about reliability, you could always add an extended warranty. Coverage for 6 or 7 years will cost you about $1,000.00 more. So instead of leasing a new car for another monthly payment of $369.84, just buy the warranty for an additional $25.00 per month and start to build some assets.

Try to plan for life changes before considering a lease. Are you looking for a new job that may change your driving habits? (The amount of mileage you drive per year is important when you consider leasing a car.) Are there upcoming circumstances that may affect your monthly budget? The vehicle looks great but will you be able to afford it during the full term of the lease?

If you are going to lease, look for a vehicle that holds it value or has a good residual value (the higher the number the better). Japanese and European vehicles tend to have better residual values than American made vehicles. Ensure your lease agreement has a fixed "buy out" or "pay off" figure (pre-determined price if you choose to purchase) at the end of the termed agreement. You can always try to negotiate a lower buy out price when the time comes. If the market value is much higher than the buy out price, you may want to consider purchasing a vehicle that you liked, even though you were not planning to buy the vehicle. As always, shop around and apply the same buying skills to obtain the best price in the first place. Negotiate the best price before you tell the dealer you plan to lease the vehicle. If you definitely do not plan to buy the vehicle at the end and it is a closed-end lease, try to negotiate a higher residual value. This will lower your monthly payment amount.

Other Items

Another way to use these skills is when buying large items around the house, doing home improvements, or adding an addition. Actually, you could apply these skills to almost anything, or any service you buy or pay for.

For my next example, I want to research replacing my asphalt driveway. I need to decide whether to replace it, repair it, or use some other material to do the job. As I have said before you should always keep your options open. While researching projects, I learn something new all the time. Acting and speaking like the people you are dealing with prevents them from taking advantage of you. In fact, when they see you are knowledgeable, they tend to give you more information and ideas.

I have many questions that need to be answered and I guess I could start by calling all of the different contractors out to my house, but that is going to take a lot of time. Not to mention, most of them usually do not show up on time or at all. I picked up the yellow pages and turned to the section for concrete contractors. I picked one out of the book to call. (I placed a dot next to the name to keep track of whom I have called already.) When they answered the phone, I explained that I had a driveway that needed replacing but I was not sure at this time what I wanted to do. I just wanted to get some estimates at this time. He explained some of my options, how the work is done, and what I should look for when I get the job done. I then asked him what I could do to get the estimate over the phone. He told me I could call him back with measurements of the driveway and he would be able to give me the figures over the phone. I also found out that I had choices of asphalt, concrete, or stamped concrete, which required different contractors. I went outside to measure the driveway.

I called the person back and gave them the measurements. He was able to tell me that I had 1,243 Square feet of driveway area that needed replacing. I asked him how he would go about installing a concrete driveway at his own home. I got all of the answers that I needed.

I then called another company that performs concrete work. I asked them the same questions and compared the answers. (If I note any discrepancies, I ask them more about it.) I gave them the same measurements and they came up with the same square footage. I now know what I need to ask all of the other contractors. If there had been any discrepancies between what the first two contractors told me, I would have called another contractor.

Now that I know what needs to be done I wait until most businesses are closed and then begin to call them, hoping they have some type of voice mail or answering machine. I call them one by one and then place a dot next to their name. I left each one the following information:

"Hi my name is _____. I live at (address, city, state, & zip code). I am looking to have my driveway replaced. I presently have an asphalt driveway that measures _____ square feet. I am looking to have a four-inch base of stone with 6 inches of finished 3500-PSI (Pounds per Square Inch) concrete. I would also like to have 5-inch mesh. Please provide me with the total cost for the job, which should include all materials, labor, excavations & disposal, cleanup, etc. I can be reached at my home number between _____PM -_____PM daily, or at my work number during the day from _____ AM - _____PM, Monday through Friday. I am calling other businesses for quotes, so please provide me with your best price. Hope to hear from you soon. Have a nice day."

I followed the same process with all of the other contractors. I even went as far as calling a concrete supplier and gave them the dimensions of the driveway. I then asked them what it would cost to have 6 inches of concrete delivered. The company gave me a price of $1,752.00 just for the concrete. Over the course of the next few days I received many return calls. Most of the representatives gave me their bottom price while others wanted further clarification on the work. Almost one-half of them never returned my call, not that I was surprised. At this point I had received the following range in prices for the different jobs.

Just the price of concrete	$1,752.00
Asphalt - partial replacement	$1,400.00 - $3,319.00
Asphalt - total replacement	$3,900.00 - $6,114.00

Concrete - total replacement	$5,593.00 - $13,979.00
Concrete stamped (total price)	$12,000.00

I only got one quote because there are limited contractors that do this work.

As you can see, the price range is all over the place. After you get the lowest bid and decide on the type of job you want done, call the person out to the house to go over the details in depth. Have them put everything in writing, no exceptions. Ask them about forms of payment, and what is required once you make a commitment. After my initial deposit, when else do I have to make a payment (when they put you on the schedule, start the work, completion of work, etc.)? When can they start the work and how long will it take to complete it once they get started? Never pay anyone more than half of the total before the job is finished. In fact, the less you can agree on the more you have in your favor should something go wrong.

In my case, I selected the lowest concrete bid of $5,593.00. (Many people feel if they choose the lowest priced job, they will receive inferior work or product. That is not true. I know many people over the years that paid a lot more and received inferior work.) However, I quickly learned I did not do my homework well enough. It turns out these contractors need to bring some heavy machinery that they do not like to transport more than twenty miles from their business, because of the cost and risk involved. This contractor declined the job after all because he was located over twenty-five miles away. All of the other companies were within 10 miles of my home. The next lowest bid was $12,740.00. That is $7,147.00 more than the previous business.

Why should there be such a difference in pricing? I could either go with them or use the low figure to go back and bargain with the others. Or I may just go back and call some of the contractors that never returned my call the first time. I could also wait until it is slow season. How do you know that? Just ask them. Many times when businesses are very busy they give high bids because they do not need the work. Some businesses do not even do the work themselves; they subcontract it out to other contractors. Therefore, you end up paying them both. Always ask the people you are about to do business with if they perform the work themselves or do they subcontract it out.

Eliminate the middleman unless you are doing a major job that requires multiple trades. Sometimes it is needed and a good thing, if you are building a house or a major addition on your home. The whole point of this chapter is that you can apply these skills to any type of service or product you must pay for. You would have saved $7,132.00 just on my last real life experience alone, unless you got lucky and contacted the lowest priced contractor the first time. You will not be lucky all the time.

From time to time you may want to purchase an item that may have limited local market share in your area. Because of that, many businesses tend to charge top dollar because they do not have competition. One example would be stainless steel barbecue grills. If you shop around in your local area for a specific manufacturer's grill, you would probably be lucky if you found five dealers within a fifty-mile radius. This is how I handle these situations. I go to the store where I first saw the grill and ask for the literature that they have on the product. If they do not have any, I ask them if I could see the owner's manual. You will be able to find the model number of the grill, along with the list of options you would like, company name, address, city, state, and phone number. Sometimes the company name will be different from the company name on the product. Always look for the toll-free numbers first, and then write down others just in case the toll-free number is no longer valid. If you were not able find a toll-free number, try to obtain one by calling toll-free directory assistance. Call the manufacturer and let them know you are looking to purchase their product and provide them with the model number.

Ask them if they can provide you with the names of businesses in your area that sell that item. If you only get three or four names of businesses, I would also ask for alternate businesses in nearby states. Sometimes they will only give you a few names on the phone and you may have to call back a few hours later for the rest. Ask them if they can mail you a complete list. Tell the manufacturer you desire to purchase the grill at a good price and if they could recommend one or two of their distributors that sell their products at a lower price. You can probably get this information on the Internet. Once you have all of the information you are ready to get started and save some money.

Example 3:   Wish to purchase a new stainless steel grill. (Original price at first store was $6,355.00)

1.   The first thing you want to do is create a list complete with the price of the grill, and all accessories that you are considering purchasing.

2.   Start by calling the business that is farthest away from your home. When someone answers, ask for the owner. Get his/her name and let them know you are looking to purchase a grill made by (manufacturer's name). Provide the representative with all of the parts from your list, along with the model number. Tell him/her the reason you are calling is that you are looking for the lowest price. Let the person know you are a very good negotiator and are willing to come to their location to pick up the grill. Give him/her your phone number and ask them to get back to you. Make him/her aware you have already received some good prices and you will go with the lowest price.

3.   Wait until someone calls you back. It should take a few hours or a day at the most. If the price you are quoted is less than a thousand dollars from the original price, lower the original price by $1,200.00* (to $5,155.00). Tell him/her you already received a better price of $5,155.00. The person may say this price is lower than what the store pays for it. Then say, "You're kidding," and pause. Ask the person, "What do these items cost

you?" See if you can get the breakdown of each one. Keep in mind that their wholesale price may be higher than other stores who sell more of that product line. The person may come back and say he/she can beat the price by another $50.00.

4. In either case, go back through paragraph 2. I would call at least two more businesses and see what they are offering. Once you seem to be in the ballpark of ($5,105.00), lower your price another $200.00, which will bring you to $4,905.00. Call another place and see if they can beat or match this price. If you do not have many places to call on your list, you can also go back to a previously called business and say you realized you had made a mistake, because you had included delivery and tax in the price that you gave them. Just keep doing this until you get the bottom price. If your offer is ever too low just say, "Maybe the other place made a mistake. What is your cost for each item?"

5. Once you have the best price, look at what businesses are close to your home. Select the one that you would like to deal with. Call them up and ask for the owner. Let the owner know you are looking to purchase a grill by (manufacturer's name). Give him/her the model number and lists of parts you wish to purchase. Let the owner know you are a very good negotiator and have already gotten a fantastic price. Tell the owner you prefer to deal with him/her because it is a local business. Let the owner know your best price and let him/her know you would like them to beat it or match it. **The bottom line - I was able to save $1,590.00 on my new grill.**

*When choosing a price to quote, in other circumstances, consider the overall price of the product and choose accordingly. A certain percentage does not always apply.

Helpful Hints / Comments:

Vehicles

When buying a car, always make the salesperson aware that you are considering his/her vehicle as well as another manufacturer's vehicle. Tell him/her it will depend on where you get the best deal. (Never act like the kid in the candy store. Make the salesperson believe that you could take it or leave it.) You need to act as if you are always in charge.

Some dealers charge one or two percent for advertising. This charge is usually based on the particular vehicle, and must be paid by all dealers in the region.

Do not feel bad for the dealer when you are trying to get the bottom price. Many dealers also receive a cash incentive for each car that they sell. (Many times referred to as the holdback program, the dealers get this money back after they sell the car. It can range from one to four percent.) Other times, manufacturers offer incentives for meeting sales and volume targets. The average consumer is usually not made aware of most of these incentives. There are independent companies that will let you know what incentives are being offered at the time of inquiry. Some companies are much better than others are, so do some research. These companies charge a fee, from ten to thirty-five dollars, but it is well worth it. Some dealers receive incentives that other dealers do not, so it is important to shop around. I have found that many salespersons do not know about the dealer incentives. I guess management is trying not to share their profit with their own people.

Chapter 2

Many car dealerships like to play games and wear you down. The salesperson will try to do this by going back and forth to his/her manager for approvals. He/she will try to keep you there as long as possible. The dealership sometimes brings on one salesperson after another, trying to see if the other can help. Your salesperson tries to act like your friend when he says he is going to talk to his manager to try to get you a better deal. Many times they leave you alone in the office and leave the intercom on so they can hear what you are discussing with your friend or spouse, etc., from another location. So do not say anything you do not want them to hear. You could have it planned that you will say something like, "If this dealer doesn't give me the deal in the next few minutes we are going to leave and take the other guy's offer." This is how you can play the game. Use these tactics in your favor. Once you are an experienced negotiator, you can tell them you are there to make a deal and not to waste your time with their tactics.

Never give them a deposit until they have agreed to your price, and you see the figures and all of the options you chose listed in writing. The sales manager should sign the paperwork.

I would say that if you buy a vehicle that costs about $25,000.00 and pay $200.00 to $500.00 over the dealer's cost, you did OK. Expect to pay more for higher priced vehicles. (Remember you can make the deal for $50.00 over cost, but you are going to have to work hard for it, and the timing has to be right.)

Do not get caught up in those extra dealer packages that are add-ons. This can boost up the price by hundreds or thousands of dollars. Most of the time they are not needed. If you do want them, they can usually be purchased much cheaper after you buy the vehicle (pinstripes, upholstery protector, rust proofing, paint protection, *window etching*, etc.).

If you are looking to save additional money, you could look for a *demo* with about 3,000 to 5,000 miles on it, or purchase last year's model.

Make sure you verify the Vehicle Identification Number (VIN) is the same on the car and your paperwork, before signing the sales contract at the dealership. If you are not taking the vehicle on the day you sign the contract, write down the mileage on the odometer and ask them not to use the vehicle for any other demonstrations. Check the VIN again when you pick up the vehicle. You want to make sure they did not switch the car. The VIN is located on an engraved metal strip. It can usually be found on the dashboard against the windshield. All cars have this 17-digit identification number, which consists of numbers and letters.

If you have an extended warranty for your car, make sure to follow the manufacturer's procedures before having any work done. If you do not you could be stuck paying the bill. Most companies like to approve the work and cost before the work is completed.

If you lease or take a loan out on your vehicle, you may want to consider *Guaranteed Auto Protection* (GAP) insurance.

Check to see if the manufacturer or dealer is offering any customer rebates or incentives. Other rebates come in the form of low interest rates, zero down, or no interest for a year. (Most cars that are in demand usually do not offer these from the manufacturer.) Some manufacturers have a customer loyalty program. They give you a rebate for being a previous or existing owner of one of the manufacturer's cars. Some manufacturers will give you a rebate if you just graduated from high school and are going on to college.

You can buy extended warranties directly from the issuing insurance company and save money. Just make sure you look for a plan that covers all the parts on your vehicle. Look for a policy that says bumper-to-bumper coverage for breakdown and wear and tear issues. Ensure you are dealing with a reliable company that is well rated with the Better Business Bureau and Standard & Poor. I recommend a $0.0 or $25.00 deductible. It should include towing and a rental if the car needs to be in the shop for more than one day. Look for warranties that are transferable. Buy a warranty plan that starts the day you buy the car. Save all receipts in case you need to show proof of following the regular scheduled maintenance plan. Read the plans really well and watch for the exclusion clause. Some items that are regularly excluded from extended warranty plans are; body parts of the car, brake pads, windows, interior, battery, paint, muffler & pipes, bulbs, and any other component that was added to the car after it was purchased.

If the vehicle you are trying to buy is a hot model or in short supply, the dealer may not want to give you as much of a discount. Be patient and search around for your best deal. Tell them you are willing to wait, and be prepared to leave. Remember, you need to be in control.

When dealers get vehicles from other dealers they may have to pay a small fee of about one hundred dollars. It is usually free, except for providing a driver to go get the vehicle.

You will need the Certificate of Title (also referred to as the "pink slip") to sell or trade your vehicle. This is your official proof that you are the owner of the vehicle. Keep track of who holds the title (either yourself or the finance company). If you financed the vehicle, your lien holder keeps the title until you have paid off the loan. Make certain they send the title to you once the loan is paid in full.

Do not purchase a warranty with a longer term than the length of time you intend to keep the vehicle. For example, do not buy an extended warranty with 3 year/36,000 mile coverage if you trade in your vehicle every two years.

A very expensive extended warranty may indicate a vehicle with possible repair history problems.

Below is a list of Web sites that will help make your car buying or selling much easier. These sites range from car pricing for new and used, dealers offers, leases, loans, rebates, driver test reports, side by side vehicle comparisons, crash tests, safety tests, gasoline consumption, warranties, and many other interesting facts. If you look through these sites you will also find links to many other good sites. You should determine which sites are good for you. There are many other sites out there. You just need to look. These sites were all working as of the day this chapter was being written.

www.NADAguides.com
www.IntelliChoice.com
www.vmrintl.com
www.CarSmart.com
www.InvoiceDealers.com
www.CarsDirect.com
www.Stoneage.com
www.Cars.com
www.VehiclesOnline.com
www.HighwaySafety.org
www.LemonaidCars.com
www.CarFax.com
www.nhtsa.dot.gov
www.LendingTree.com
www.AutoCreditFinders.com
www.nhtsa.gov/cars/problems/salvage
www.1SourceAutoWarranty.com

www.Edmunds.com
www.KBB.COM
www.CarMax.com
www.CarPoint.com
www.AutoWeb.com
www.Autobytel.com
www.AutoVantage.com
www.CostcoAuto.com
www.WarrantyDirect.com
www.AutoSafety.org
www.AutoCheck.com
www.FuelEconomy.gov
www.PeopleFirst.com
www.E-Loan.com

Chapter 2

When driving a new vehicle it is important to follow the manufacturers' breaking in procedures. This will contribute to the vehicle's economical operation, durability and increase the engine's longevity. Most manufacturers set limits on: how fast you drive; quick starts; hard stops; towing a trailer; engine idling; and varying speed from time to time. Manufacturers' break in periods can range from the first 500 miles to 1500 miles. For example, if you perform hard stops during the break in period the brake shoes or pads can become glazed and affect overall function. The brakes will also wear out prematurely. Breaking your car in properly will result in better gas mileage as well.

Leasing

The Web sites below will assist you with leasing terms, laws, and calculations.

www.ACVL.com
www.ftc.gov/bcp/menu-auto.htm
www.federalreserve.gov/pubs/leasing/
www.fdic.gov/regulations/compliance/manual/part3/p3-g1.pdf
www.creditexpert.com/creditexpert/creditmanager/017_9_cm_l easebuy.jsp

Avoid wear and tear charges on leased vehicles by keeping them properly maintained. Have the dealer specify in writing exactly what the financing company means by excessive wear and tear before you sign if you are responsible for these types of charges. If you disagree with the value that the dealer has calculated at the end of your lease, consider obtaining a second opinion from another dealer, or check with an independent appraiser. The Federal Consumer Act (CLA) sets limits for what a dealer may charge for reasonable wear and tear.

Always read the fine print on your lease agreement before signing. Watch for hidden charges, such as security deposits, lease-end service fees, destination charges, and registration fees. Ask the salesperson to show you the documented residual value for your vehicle (the Automotive Lease Guide and Black Book are good resources, see if the dealer has one). The issuing bank or leasing company normally determines the residual value and may sometimes over inflate this figure. A higher residual value on your contract, than in the book, is a good deal if you do not plan to buy the vehicle. Some manufacturers artificially inflate the residual values on certain models that are not selling well to reduce the monthly payments. This is called a "subvented lease." Are there any charges that you must pay when the lease reaches it term? The dealer must tell you what type of insurance coverage you are required to keep in order to comply with the lease agreement.

Lease payments normally consist of interest, taxes, service fees, luxury fees, acquisition fees, and depreciation costs. Depreciation is calculated as the difference between the purchase price ("capitalized cost" or "cap cost") and the residual value (this is the estimated value of the vehicle at the end of term.) The interest rate portion is usually referred to as the "money factor," or "lease factor," and is shown as a decimal number. To determine your annual interest rate you need to multiply the money factor by 2400. Example, if your money factor is .0027, multiply by 2400 to obtain the annual interest rate of 6.48%.

Your monthly payments will be lower when you lease a vehicle rather than purchase that same vehicle. However, remember to include other hidden monthly and recurring costs in your budget. In Pennsylvania, there is a 9% tax on leased vehicles vs. a 6% tax on purchased vehicles. (Check the tax rates in your area.) The finance company will likely require more expensive insurance coverage than you would normally purchase. You must obtain new license plates and registration with each new lease term if you change finance companies.

Three types of maintenance plans are available when leasing. The first is a "non-maintenance lease" in which you are responsible for the maintenance and repairs. The second is a "maintenance lease" in which the dealer is responsible for the cost, but you will need to take the vehicle to their repair shops. The last type is a "budget maintenance lease." In this type, you pay a set monthly fee into an account that will be used to cover all repair costs. When the vehicle term is up you will receive a refund for any money left over in that account, or you may owe if the account falls short. Any costs for maintenance and repairs should be taken into account before signing the lease. Some cars require frequent maintenance and the parts may be expensive.

Lease a vehicle for the amount of time the vehicle is covered under the manufacturer's warranty, usually 3 years. This way you will not incur expenses for breakdowns.

Never sign an open-end lease agreement. (May be good if you are a business owner.) You will be responsible for the difference in the depreciation value if it is less than the originally calculated estimated residual value. Look for a closed-end lease (walk-away) which allows you to return the vehicle at the end of the term without worrying about value depreciation.

Make sure your contract allows for early termination should you need it. In the event you terminate the lease early, how will they determine your mileage for that term?

Try to avoid lease-end excess mileage charges by increasing your mileage allowance before you enter the agreement. Renegotiate your mileage rate if you plan to drive substantially fewer miles than the lease agreement allows. Vehicles with less mileage are worth more to the finance company when the lease is over.

If you plan to lease a vehicle, the strategy for obtaining the best price in the off-season does not always apply. You may be charged more to compensate for vehicles the dealer has lost money on as they sat on the lot.

If the leasing company does not offer a fixed buy out, or gap insurance, walk away from the deal.

Do not sublease your vehicle because you are ultimately responsible for all damages.

If you are hard on your vehicle, you should not consider leasing.

Ask the dealer what types of leases are available. Have them explain the differences, along with the advantages and disadvantages.

It is often possible to transfer the license plate from one leased vehicle to the next. Double check with the dealer even if they say no the first time you ask.

If you decide to purchase the vehicle at the end of your lease agreement, you will usually end up spending more overall than if you had financed the car originally. Sometimes you get lucky and lease a vehicle with a market value close to what you paid after your 3-year term is up, yet your buy out price is substantially lower. In this case, I recommend you buy the car from the dealer, even if you just plan to sell it or use it as a trade.

It can be difficult to confirm that the monthly lease payment you are quoted is correct. Many calculations are used to determine this figure. Some people can actually be charged the full sticker price after they have negotiated a lower price. Mistakes in math, proper credit for your rebate or trade, other hidden charges, and even intentional mistakes can be at fault. The following formulas can be used to determine what your monthly payment should be once you have the numbers explained below.

Cap Cost – Cap Cost Reductions = Net Cap Cost
Residual Percentage × MSRP = Residual
(Net Cap Cost – Residual) ÷ Term = Monthly Depreciation
(Net Cap Cost + Residual) × Money Factor = Finance Charge
Monthly Depreciation + Finance Charge = Monthly Payment
Monthly Payment + Your local Taxes = Total Monthly Payment

Glossary of terms
Cap Cost - The price you are paying for the vehicle, any prior loan balances, and luxury taxes.
Cap Cost Reductions - down payment, trade-in, incentives, and rebates.
Money Factor - This a decimal number provided by the dealer or finance company.
MSRP - The actual sticker price of the vehicle.
Residual - This is a percentage of the MSRP.
Residual Percentage - This a percentage provided by the dealer or finance company.

Example
I will make the following assumptions.
You lease a vehicle with an MSRP of $24,000.00 (sticker price) for a 36-month term. You have a trade worth $5,000.00, a down payment of $2,000.00, and you were able to negotiate a lower price of $22,000.00 (Cap Cost) on the vehicle. There were no prior loan balances, rebates, or incentives.
Your dealer told you that your money factor is .0025 and your Residual Percentage is 55%.

$22,000 negotiated price – $5,000 trade – $2,000 down
payment = $15,000 Net Cap Cost
55% residual percentage × $24,000 MSRP or invoice
price = $13,200 Residual
($15,000 net cap cost - $13,200 residual) ÷ 36 month term
= $50.00 Monthly Depreciation
($15,000 net cap cost + $13,200 residual) × .0025 money
factor = $70.50 Finance Charge
$50.00 monthly depreciation + $70.50 finance charge =
$120.50 Monthly Payment
$120.50 monthly payment + 9% (or your local tax
percentage) = $131.34 Total Monthly Payment

Other Items

Many contractors or salespeople will try to make you feel
guilty because you are offering them low prices. They
may say things like, "I will not be able to feed my
children" or, "I have another customer interested in the
same product." Stay in control and say, "It's up to you,
this is my offer." Do not let them get to you. Be calm and
friendly, but do not let them waste your time. Try to keep
a smile on your face. If they tell you that it cannot be
done, or they cannot match your price, just respond,
"Maybe you don't want my business but others will."

Put the deposit on a credit card just in case you should
change your mind. Many times the credit card companies
will recover your deposit if you dispute the charge.

If you are considering a major project around your home
such as new siding, windows, driveway, or landscaping,
consider speaking to your neighbors and see if they have a
similar interest. If more than one neighbor uses the same
contractor you should be able to get further discounts. Do
not let the contractor know about the others until you have
gotten the best price for your job. This way you can see if
he/she is giving you a better deal for multiple jobs.

If you are the first one to build something in your neighborhood you can usually negotiate a better price. This is because people will see the product or service performed and would question who did the work. This has the potential for future business. Let the contractor know that you will refer business to them as people inquire about the work.

Before selecting a contractor, check the following things:
Make sure the company is fully licensed and insured, and that they offer a warranty on their work. What is their license number? If an uninsured contractor, or any of his employees, gets hurt on your property, you could be liable for the medical bills. Likewise, you could be faced with the expense of repairing any damage to your property resulting from an improperly performed installation.

Will they ensure the job will be done safely and correctly (in compliance with city building codes), and will it be inspected by the appropriate agency, if needed? Will the contractor take care of permits, if needed? If you live in a city where a permit is required and the contractor does not secure one, you may be required to have the job done over, even if it was done properly.

Get in writing both the manufacturer's and the contractor's warranties on the equipment and installation. The manufacturer's warranty should specify the length of time your unit is covered and which of the specific components are included.

What are the prices and terms? The contractor should provide you with a written contract before performing the work. Make sure the quoted price includes all the equipment, labor, installation, permits, and taxes. Ask them if they Sub-Contract any of the work. Know exactly who will be doing the work.

Make sure they have been in business for a while and they are not a fly by night company. Ask for references for similar jobs they have done in your area, so you can see their work. (Do not just ask for the references, but actually follow-up on a few. Ask the people if they had any issues, no matter how small.) Also, check with the local Better Business Bureau to see if the company is in good standing.

Chapter 3

Customer Service Issues

This is one of my favorite subjects. It is amazing how many issues we run into in the course of our daily lives. I will touch on a few, but as usual, you can apply these skills to any situation.

I would like to know what happened to the time when a handshake meant something, or when you called a company and they gave you the correct answer the first time. Today, if you call a company three times and ask the same question, you will probably get three different answers.

If you make a mistake on your credit card, checking, or other account, you are penalized with a fee. If your bill is late, if you want a copy of your check statement, if you have overdraft protection and use it, or if you go over your credit limit, there is a charge. If they really did not want you to go over your maximum balance, they could easily stop you. This is the age of computers. Instead, they hope you do so they can charge you another twenty-five dollars for being such a good customer.

Just recently I had to deal with an issue. I called the company's customer service number and got their voice response system. I listened to eight or nine options and was asked to make a choice. Then I was given about five more options and asked to make another choice. After two more rounds of selections, I finally got a message that said the company was closed and to please call back during normal business hours. It was after 9:00 AM on the East Coast. I guess the company was located on the West Coast, but I will never know because the message did not even give their normal business hours. Great customer service. The company could have given me a message before I went through all of the options. I bet if I had called that same company to place an order, I would only have had to wait a few minutes. I think companies like to create as many hurdles as possible to prevent you from calling. In fact, the last time I had a similar experience, I went through three or four levels of the voicemail system, only to be disconnected. I called back again and the same thing occurred. If you complain to the businesses about these systems, they say they are being installed to improve customer service. Who are they kidding? They are just looking to cut down on their expenses, which in turn creates problems for the consumer.

Do you ever keep track of how long these companies keep you on hold? Well I have, and I cannot believe that people actually hold on for that long. Once I turned on my speakerphone while I was watching TV. I listened to their recording as the minutes ticked by. I actually waited about fifty minutes. Unbelievably, when I finally got through, the person's computer system went down and they could not help me. They asked me to call back. I was furious. I asked the person if they could call me back, transfer me to another number, or give me an alternate number to call so I would not have to wait on hold again. She just replied, "I'm sorry sir, I can't do that. You'll have to call back." She hung up before I could say another word.

My favorite is when I call to speak to someone about a problem with one of my accounts. I am calling because I want to discuss an issue with a real live person. When I call, I get their voice response system. "Please listen to the entire message because our menus have changed. Please make one of the following selections so we can serve you faster." I make a selection and then I am asked to punch in my account number. After I do that, I am asked for the last four digits of my social security number. There is a pause and then, all of a sudden, the computer begins to tell me about my account balance, last payment, and other things I already know. All I want is to get to a person to ask them a question. I finally tired of listening to it all and pressed the "0" key. I heard my call being transferred. Two to three minutes later someone answers the phone and asks if they can help me. I said, "I would like to talk to you about my account." The person asked me for my account number. "I just entered all that information, don't you see it." They say, "No, we don't see that information. Can I please have your account number?" So I had to start all over again after I had just wasted at least 5 minutes of my time and now I am aggravated before I even speak to the person. Have you noticed that all the people who answer the phones nowadays have "manager" in their title (account manager, executive manager, etc.)? Is that to make us feel better?

Changes should help the customer as well as the company. In reference to my example when I had to enter my social security number, I should have been given the option to listen to my balance, or to speak to a customer service representative. When I finally was transferred, they should only have had to verify my name, etc., to ensure I was not lost in the call transfers. They should have already had my account information in front of them.

So, you ask, what can you do now? Where do you go from here? The first step is to start writing letters to these companies and spread the word to your family, friends, and neighbors. This will not be an easy task, but with time, the world will start to change for the better. The second step is to start looking out for yourself and ensure that companies do not take advantage of you. If they do, you need to start to charge them for your time. Think about it this way. If you owned your own business and had to spend time on the phone with companies to deal with their mistakes or issues, you would lose valuable work time. Your time is money. How many times have you called to resolve an issue only to end up more aggravated with the situation? Someone should be responsible to pay you for the aggravation.

This does not apply to cases such as if your telephone bill has a mistake and you have to call them to resolve it. As long as they resolve the error the first time and were pleasant, you would not charge them for that. If the person was not as pleasant as you thought he/she should be, or just did not seem to ask the right questions, ensure that you have the person's name or employee number. Request to speak to his/her manager and make them aware of the situation. This is how you will contribute to making this world a better place. The big problem today is we all just let it go instead of informing someone. The goal is not to try to get the person fired or reprimanded, but to have them trained better in the first place. This way, your next call, or someone else's, will be more pleasant. If the person continues to be that way, and complaints keep coming in, the manager will probably take further action. Some companies actually prefer to receive this type of feedback than have a dissatisfied customer. Now, if the manager does not see anything wrong and you really did have an issue, I would escalate it again to that person's manager. Just remember to get the name or ID number. Be certain that you are not in the wrong.

Example 1:   Let us take this past situation and twist it around a little bit. Maybe you called the telephone company a second time because your problem was not resolved after the first phone call. Your bill still shows the same mistake, and now it says that your payment is late.

When the person answers the phone, ask for his/her name and telephone extension. If the person tells you they cannot give you that information, ask for his/her employee number. Mark the date and time of your call next to his/her name on a sheet of paper. At this point, make the person aware this is the second time you are calling about this matter. Inform them of the date of your previous call, along with the name of the person with whom you spoke. Tell them you had been assured the problem would be resolved. At this point, this conversation can go one of three ways.

1) *The problem has been resolved.* The person says they are very sorry for the inconvenience and the correction has taken place, even though it has not shown up on the bill. The reason your bill

does not show the correction is that the change went in after the billing statements went to print. The person you spoke with last should have told you this. They give you the correct figure you should pay. Again the person apologizes for the mistake. At this point ask that person to send you a letter stating that you were not late on your bill, that it was the company's error. You will need this letter if there is ever a question in the future regarding this incident on your credit report.

2) *The problem has not been resolved but the representative acknowledges you were inconvenienced. She is doing everything possible to fix things for you.* The person says they are very sorry for the inconvenience. That person sees that you called before, but for some reason the change did not happen. The person is so sorry you had to be inconvenienced again. Your next bill will show the correction. The person will recheck your account in a few weeks to ensure it goes through this time. They give you the correct figure you should pay. Again the person apologizes for the mistake. At this point ask them to send you a letter that you were not late on your bill, that it was the company's error.

3) *The problem has not been resolved and you are being treated poorly.* The person says they do not have a record of your prior call, and they insist they keep track of all calls. Tell them you definitely spoke to (name of person) on (date of previous call). The person told you that your problem would be resolved.

Ask for the person's supervisor. Either he/she will pass you on at this time, or they will tell you they can resolve your problem. Tell them the last person told you that your problem would be resolved, it is now a month later, and you are still trying to get the issue resolved. You have wasted your time, not to mention the aggravation the company has caused you. At this point request that the person get the supervisor again. If the person continues to talk and not get the supervisor, ask them, "Are you refusing to transfer me to a supervisor?" He/she may be silent or insist that they can help. Demand to speak to a supervisor or else you will hang-up and call back. By this time you will either be transferred or you will have to call back.

If you do have to call back, make sure you get the name or ID number and extension of the person who answers the phone. Tell that person that you had a problem with one of his/her co-workers and you only want to speak to a supervisor or a manager. You will have to give them your name and account number. Sometimes the person wants to know the details of the problem. Tell him/her you are tired of repeating yourself and would like to speak to a supervisor.

At this point you should be able to speak to the supervisor. (Get the supervisor's name or ID, phone number & extension and mark down the date and time called.) You should let the supervisor know how upset you are over this issue, and that one of their employees gave you a hard time and refused your request to escalate the matter. Remind the supervisor that the first person you dealt with never resolved the issue. Tell them the reason you wanted to speak with them was to ensure that the problem is resolved this time. You also want to be compensated for your aggravation. Explain your problem to the supervisor and tell them to make certain that they resolve it. Ask them to send you a letter that you were not late on your bill, that it was the company's error.

Remind the supervisor you wish to be compensated for the aggravation their staff and company have put you through. You want your account credited for twenty-five dollars. That is a small price for them to pay considering what you had to go through. Your time is worth money, and you expect the company to pay you for your time. If he/she says they cannot do that, tell the person they should get someone on the phone that can authorize it, or have them call you back. If you have to hang up, first ask for his manager's name and extension, in case you have to call them back. Ask them for a commitment on when they will get back to you. Tell the supervisor that if this continues and you do not hear back from them, they will need to pay you even more.

If no one calls you back, call the highest-level manager directly and explain the whole situation. Let them know you had originally requested twenty-five dollars, but you are now requesting fifty dollars. Tell the supervisor that if this matter is not resolved this time, you will expect additional compensation.

Always be polite throughout these conversations. Use the words "please" and "thank you" where appropriate, even if the other person is rude to you. Do not yell because it will only make the person on the other end become more aggressive. Do not back down on your request. However, you may need to compromise on the dollar amount. You need to be fair about your request. Remember to keep cool, because when it is all over, you will have the issue resolved and you will be paid for your time and aggravation. You will not be as aggravated when it comes to dealing with problems in the future. You will start to look at these issues as opportunities to contribute constructive criticism and improve their business, while being paid for it.

Example 2:   Before I get into the next example let me set the mood. You get together with two other couples each year to celebrate your mutual anniversary. You plan ahead and choose a nice restaurant. This is a very important night for all of you. When you arrive at the restaurant at 7:00 PM, you notice some of the silverware is a little dirty. When you place your order, the waitperson informs you that one of the items that two people wanted to order is not available. Before the food even arrives, the dining room becomes overwhelmed with noise from the band playing in the next room. Everyone at the table has to talk very loud just to be heard. It is also getting to be very warm in the room. During the meal, half of the table is pleased, while the other half is not thrilled with the food. You mention most of these items to the waiter, who apologizes multiple times. The waiter provides some legitimate excuses. Throughout the meal, most of you keep focusing on all of the issues rather than your purpose for being there. Your night is ruined. What should you do?

By all rights if you run into a situation like this, the manager or maître d' should seek out your table without your asking to speak to them, in response to the dissatisfaction you expressed to the waitperson.

1. If the manager shows up and asks what the problems are, explain all of the issues to them. Let them know how important this night was to you and that both the meal and the evening were ruined for all of you.

2. A good manager will be very apologetic and ask what he/she can do to salvage your evening. At this point ask, "What could you do, because it did ruin our dinner and ambience?"

3. Some managers will offer you dessert and coffee, on the house. I do not think this is fair when most of the night is ruined and you still have to pay a hefty dinner check. Let them know how you feel. The offer is nice but it does not make up for the aggravation. The manager may ask you what you would like at this time. Tell him/her you prefer to

be asked back, as their guest, so that they can make it up to you.

4.   Most managers will probably try to compromise and take a bottle or two of wine off your bill, along with the desserts, or they may invite you back for brunch, as their guest.

5.   You could either accept their offer at this time, or just say that you do not want to make this night any worse than it is already, and you will follow up with them later in the week. Get his/her name and phone number.

This is a good idea because you and the manager have time to think about it. Most managers will still give you the desserts on the house. When it comes to leaving the tip, if the service was good, take off just a few dollars because of the problems. If the waiter was nice overall, do not penalize them completely.

6.   Sometime within a few days of the incident, call the manager. Let him/her know again how it ruined your night and tell him/her that you would like to all be invited back as their guest. Most of the time the manager will do that. If not, request to speak to his/her management, or to the owner of the restaurant. Explain the situation to the owner and repeat your request. Do not back down, even if it causes you aggravation, because you paid for the meal and are entitled to good food, a pleasant atmosphere, and good service. After all, that is why you go out for dinner. Most people do not say anything about a bad experience and it frustrates them later.

The Insider's Guide to Saving Money

Stand up for your rights when you go out to dinner. Most restaurants would like the opportunity to make things right when you are dissatisfied with a meal. If you do not like what you ordered, they will often offer to bring you a different entrée of your choice. If, for some reason, you have now lost your appetite, just ask them to take it off your bill.

Example 3: The next example that I address can be applied to a variety of situations. I had decided to buy a certain camera and the best price I found was $220.00. While looking through the newspaper, I discovered a local store was advertising their cameras at $40.00 to $60.00 off. The camera that I was looking for was $60.00 off at a final price of $160.00.

The first day of the sale, my daughter and I arrived at the store just as it opened. We proceeded directly to the camera department. I asked the salesperson for the camera, but they told me they did not have that model in stock. The salesperson offered me the model below it for the same price, but I did not want that. I asked them how they could be sold out when the sale just started today and I was their first customer. The salesperson informed me they have been out of stock for a week or two, but the camera should be back in stock any day now. I asked to speak to the manager, but the manager did not appear.

I walked to the customer service desk and asked for the manager. It took the manager a long time to come out and speak to me.

1. The manager asked what the problem was. I showed her the ad and explained that they do not have the item in stock. The manager then phoned the camera department.

2. The manager hung up and said that the store does not carry this model camera at all. (This was a different story than what the salesperson told me originally.) The manager said there was nothing she could do. I suggested they should be able to

get the camera from another of their stores. The manager offered me another camera they had on sale, for only $35.00 less than the original price of $149.00. The only one of those cameras they had in stock was a demo unit. I told her I was willing to take the other camera if they ordered a new one for me, and gave me the same discount that they were offering on the first one ($60.00 off). The manager replied she could not do that. I then told the manager I wanted the original camera that their store was advertising in the paper.

3. At this point the manager raised her voice and said, "We don't carry everything they put in these ads in every store." I responded that I could understand they may not have it in the store, but they should be able to order it. I pointed out that I had already been inconvenienced because I came in for a product that they do not even have. The manager walked behind the counter. I said she could at least try to call another store to see if they have it. At this point she yelled from across the counter to get out of the store because she was tired of me being rude to her. I said, "I was not rude. You just don't know how to deal with a customer. Why are you upset with me when I'm the one who is being impacted, and I didn't do anything wrong?" I asked the manager for her supervisor's name and phone number along with the phone number for their corporate *headquarters*. There were people standing around and I kindly asked one if they felt that I was being rude. They replied that I was not. As soon as I arrived at home, I wrote down all of the things that were said in the store, while they were still fresh in my mind.

4. On Monday I called the corporate headquarters and explained the situation. I now told them I

wanted the camera for $100.00 less than the regular price, because of the aggravation and embarrassment I had to go through. They were very apologetic and said that someone would call me back. I got the representative's name and phone number and hung up.

5. Within a few hours, I received a call from the *general manager* (GM) of the store. The GM asked me what my issue was. I explained in detail from the beginning. He told me that he had a conversation with the manager, about the incident, and was told that I had been rude to her. The GM said they were willing to get the camera I wanted and would take $50.00 off the price. I told him I did not like being embarrassed in the store and I thought the manager should have handled this matter differently. The GM still kept bringing up that I may have been rude. I told him he was wrong. I told him we could resolve this issue now or I would escalate this to corporate headquarters and request the camera for free. He said that was all he was willing to do.

6. I called the corporate headquarters and explained what had taken place with the general manager and informed them I was not happy with his resolution. I wanted to escalate the matter to the next level. I got the name and phone number of the highest-level management and hung up.

7. About a half hour later the regional manager called and left a message that he had received my complaint and he will try me again later. Ten minutes later, I received a call from the store manager that I had spoken with the day before. He said he would give me the $100.00 off that I wanted. I said, "That was the offer on the table the last time we spoke. You still felt that I was wrong

and I don't think you handled the situation the right way either." I told him I now wanted the camera for free because I had to spend even more time on this matter and continued to get aggravated. He said, "I just couldn't give you the camera for free." I said, "I'll tell you what. I also need film. We can end this now if you order me a new camera and 15 rolls of 36-exposure film. I will pay you $50.00 plus tax for the camera and film in total." He said he really could not do that. I then told him I was not sure why he called me. Now my request is going to go up because you wasted more of my time when I had already escalated the matter. The GM finally agreed. The regional manager called back to confirm everything was resolved. I told him the GM and I had come to an agreement, and I thanked him for his help.

8.   I went to the store to pick up the new camera when it arrived. I also picked up my 15 rolls of film. All for only $50.00.

Yes, I did spend a bit of time on the telephone. However, in the end, I feel I was adequately compensated for my time and aggravation.

Example 4:   We have all traveled at one time or another and have found that some hotels are not quite what we expected. The following is just one reason to consult the general manager of the hotel. You should be entitled to some type of compensation for any legitimate concern that you have about your stay.

You go to a hotel to stay for three days. On the second day you stop by the room at 12:00 PM for a few minutes. Housekeeping had already finished in the room for the day. Everything was in order. When you return to the room, at about 5:00 PM, you find dirt all over the bathroom floor. You also notice dirt on the floor by the trashcan, and by the window. You are very concerned knowing someone has been in your room. You notify security and they come up to conduct an investigation. They later determine the hotel staff was not involved and could not provide an explanation. That night you have trouble sleeping because you think someone may come back into the room. You check out of the hotel the next morning. After you arrive home you call the GM and explain what happened. He checks into the matter but still could not come up with an explanation. You tell the GM you would like to be compensated for the anxiety you experienced that last day, worrying that someone had access to your room. The GM offers you a voucher to be used at any one of their hotels for a one-night stay.

Example 5:   You are standing in line at the supermarket, waiting to pay for your items. The clerk rings everything up and runs your credit card through for payment. The clerk then informs you that your credit card has been denied. You assure them you are nowhere near the credit limit on the card. The clerk tells you that his machine says you need to call the credit card company and suggests you go to the Customer Service desk. Meanwhile, your neighbor, who is checking out in the next line, asks you if you need money. You politely reply that you are fine. You pay for your purchases with another card. You then go to the service desk and they call the credit card company. The representative informs you that a hold has been placed on your account. After further discussion, you determine that there was no good reason for them to do that. When you get home you call the credit card company and ask to speak to the manager. You tell the manager what happened and that you want to be compensated for your inconvenience and embarrassment. The manager applies a fifty-dollar credit to your account.

Example 6:   With the cost of healthcare constantly going up most health maintenance organizations (HMO's) are trying to look for ways to cut costs. One of the ways they do this is by influencing the services and medication we require. I find myself fighting with my HMO more and more about the type of medication my doctor ordered. They are always trying to substitute a cheaper medication. It is not so bad if the drug they want to substitute is the generic, but nowadays they try to push the drugs that are in their formulary. Many of us find ourselves changing health insurance every few years. I do not think it is fair for these HMOs to tell us that we now have to use a different drug than we have been using for maintenance for years. If this type of issue impacts you have your doctor send a letter indicating that those drugs do not agree with your system and they do not properly control your medical problem. If that does not work, escalate the matter within your HMO and go through the appeal process. If you have a lawyer that you do not have to pay, a friendly letter addressing the matter will be enough to give them a jump-start. Also, go back to your employer and let them know about the letter the doctor sent to the insurance company and that the insurance company is giving you a hard time. Your local newspaper may be interested in doing a story.

Example 7: As I was writing this book, a member of my family told me about one of their recent experiences dealing with a customer service issue. This person would not have been able to do this in the past, but now feels comfortable dealing with these situations.

She ordered an item from one of those TV shopping channels. When the item arrived a piece was missing. She called the customer service department and was told they would try to find the missing piece and send it out to her. Three or four days later the customer service department called back and informed her they could not find the piece. They instructed her to return the item to them and they would send out a new, complete package. My family member asked if they were willing to issue partial credit if she was willing to keep the item with the missing piece. The company said they would apply a five-dollar credit to her bill. She said she would think about it and get back to them with a decision.

She then looked at the information material that came with the original package to see if she could find the manufacturer's name and phone number. She found the manufacturer's name and address and then called information to get the phone number. She explained to the manufacturer that she had just bought the item and a part was missing. They asked her for the model number and the name of the missing component. They were very apologetic and offered to send the part out immediately. She now had the issue resolved but she had wasted time to do that. (However, it was probably easier than having to pack up the old item and return it. Who knows, it is always possible that something could have been broken or missing in the new package. Not to mention that she would have waited longer to receive it.)

She called the TV shopping channel company again and asked to speak to a supervisor. She explained how she had originally called them and they were not able to resolve the issue without asking her to send the item back. She informed the supervisor that she called the manufacturer herself and that is what they should have done. She told them she wanted to be compensated twenty-five dollars for having to do their job. The supervisor apologized and gladly credited her account for the twenty-five dollars.

It goes to show you that with a little patience and determination the company could have easily resolved the problem. They could have even opened up the new box they were planning to send, taken out the one component that was originally missing, and sent it to her. The company could have made a customer happy, saved money on shipping both ways, and saved the amount of time their staff had to spend on the phone listening to the complaint. Not to mention the money they lost for compensation.

Chapter 3

Sometimes you run into large companies that will do everything possible to prevent you from escalating a complaint. If you run into a problem like this, you will have to work hard to infiltrate their system. The first thing I do is try calling the 800 number that I have at different times of day, and I try to escalate the matter to a supervisor or manager. If that does not work, call any other numbers that you may have. If the numbers you call lead you to the same customer service location try pressing "0." If there are other choices, select one of them and tell the person you would like to speak to the *vice president* or *director* who is in charge of the customer service area. If that does not work, call the customer service area and ask them where their corporate headquarters are located. Ask if their company is a part of a larger corporation or parent company. At the end of the conversation, ask them if they have a phone number for the corporate headquarters location. Sometimes you may have to tell little fibs. They may ask you why you want to know this information. Just tell them you want to do business with their company and it is personal. Try to call the numbers they give you. See if you can get in touch with the vice president or director who is in charge of the customer service area. If not, ask them to transfer you to a senior manager. Once you get to that level, explain that you have a serious customer service issue and the staff at their customer service center refused to escalate the matter. Let them know what you went through, in a sentence or two. The manager will most likely have the proper department manager or senior management call you back. Be sure to get the persons' name and number in case you should have to call back. Thank the person very much for their help.

If you were not able to get any new numbers and still have not made contact with senior management, call toll-free directory assistance and see if you can find other toll-free numbers for that company. If they have a few, you are looking for one that may say "executive management." If that does not work, call information and ask for the company's main number based on the address information you got earlier. Another thing you could try, if the phone number you are dialing is not an 800 number, is dialing the same first seven numbers and changing one of the last three digits. This will usually get you in the same company and you can tell the person who answers that you were transferred to them by accident, and they will transfer you to the correct number. One of these steps will definitely work to get around the system. Do not give up.

Example 8:   We all use services that require tipping. People seem to have different opinions on this subject. Many feel you are supposed to give people the same percentage tip, no matter what the service was like. I strongly disagree. I feel the purpose of the tip is to let the person know they did a good job. I think tipping began as a show of gratitude for the services an individual provided to you. If he/she did a fantastic job, give them more. Alternatively, if he/she did a bad job, give them less. If they just screwed up everything they did, you may even consider not leaving a tip at all. I have done that once or twice in my life. I also made sure to let the business know the reason I did not leave a tip. It is amazing how many people believe that tips should be given automatically. I strongly believe this is a way to influence our society. If one person continuously makes less than one of their counterparts, they hopefully will ask themselves why. Just think if you give them the same tip whether they provide good or bad service, how you are really showing your appreciation to these people. If we all start doing this, I think that over time, it will let people know they have to do a good job in order to receive a tip. Do not be another one of these people who walk away upset with the service you just received, yet you left a nice tip. See additional information on this topic in the "Travel" section of chapter 8.

Helpful Hints / Comments:

When dealing with voice response systems, sometimes dialing "0" at the prompt will get you to a customer service representative faster.

A very expensive extended warranty often indicates a repair history problem.

If you need to send a complaint letter, make certain you include all of the details of what transpired. Tell them what you would like them to do and by what date. If you are requesting any form of compensation, let them know what you want and why. Be very nice, and try to keep your emotions out of it. Sending a letter to a company is very powerful, in comparison to a phone call. If you are not satisfied with the results, escalate the matter to the *CEO* with other letters.

Remember that these steps do not always work. I was unsuccessful approximately three times out of about forty to fifty issues in my lifetime. You cannot win them all. Sometimes even when you are one hundred percent right, you may lose.

Ensure that you get a receipt and hang on to it. It can save you money and aggravation in the future. I like to keep mine in a folder sorted by year of purchase. If you are a homeowner, some of the receipts could save you money when you sell the property if the items were permanently installed or used to maintain the property. You will need to check your local tax laws.

If you have to mail an item back, send it the cheapest way or it will cost you more. It usually takes four or five days longer. In some cases your package will arrive in the same timeframe, even though you chose the cheaper rate.

If you are sending an expensive item back by mail or truck, make certain you insure the package against damage or theft. If the company you are sending it to is taking responsibility for the item, have them put it in writing.

If an item is just out of warranty, most companies will work with you if you escalate the matter.

I have run into many situations where I have called the corporate headquarters to register a complaint about a business, and was informed that the location was

independently owned and was a franchise. They told me
my problem would be forwarded back to the original
location. They also indicated that they really could not get
involved, other than noting the complaint, and passing it
on to the general manager of that location. They indicated
that they could not override that manager's decision. If
you are still not happy with the results go back to the
corporation and insist on speaking to the next level of
management within the customer service area. These
franchises sign agreements and the corporations can do
something if you escalate the matter high enough. Do not
take "no" for an answer.

If you are like me you have probably ordered pizza,
steaks, or other fast food products for delivery to your
home. Most of the time they arrive OK. Sometimes they
arrive cold, soggy, very late or something else may be
wrong. Call the establishment and let them know about the
problem. Tell them you would like to receive full credit
for the item, or items, on your next order, because of the
problem and inconvenience it caused you.

It is very important to have detailed notes concerning your
conversations with a company when you are trying to
resolve issues with that company.

If you have to pay for a toll call due to a customer service
issue, request reimbursement for the call.

It is very important to remember that you are not doing
this for the money. You are doing it to be compensated for
your aggravation. Hopefully, if enough people do these
things, the businesses will eventually change their
methods. At the same time, if you follow these skills, and
you run into businesses or people who go the extra mile,
let them know. Inform an exceptional worker's manager
that it is a pleasure to deal with them. Hopefully he/she
will become the role models within their organization. (If
the waiter or waitress does a fantastic job, leave them a

better tip.) The whole idea behind this is that we need to raise our expectations instead of allowing them to fall lower and lower as each year goes by.

If you have a customer service issue, and have tried everything possible to resolve the matter but have been unsuccessful, you have a few options. Contact your local Bureau of Consumer Protection, Office of the Attorney General, Small Claims Court, or even a private attorney. These Web sites may also help you.

www.naca.net   www.abanet.org

Chapter 4

Buying New Real Estate

If you are considering new construction, this tip could save you money. When visiting sample homes and new developments, do not fill out a visitor's card. Do not give your name. This will prevent them from sending you information at your residence. Sometimes they even pass on your information to other businesses that may send you junk mail. Once you give them your name, you lose the opportunity to save money. The agents may insist that you sign in, even just to walk through the sample homes. I refuse to sign the book and tell them I am working with a realtor. "The realtor recommended this area to me. We were supposed to come together next week, but I just happened to be in the area and thought I would stop in and take a peek." If they ask my realtor's name, I tell them I do not remember which realtor made the recommendation because I am working with more than one.

Once you have decided on a house, contact a real estate office and request to speak to the owner. Tell the realtor you are interested in purchasing a new construction home and have already selected a house you would like to purchase. Tell the person you would like them to represent you in your dealings with the developer. (Most developers are willing to pay realtors finders' fees. They usually range from one to three percent.) Let the realtor know you expect him/her to share the commission since you did all the work for them in finding a home to purchase. All he/she needs to do is accompany you to the model home and you will fill out a card listing the realtor as your agent. If the realtor agrees, give them the details on the property and follow his/her instructions. Many times the realtor does not even have to visit the property; it can be handled by fax. I have found that having a realtor involved can help in negotiating a slightly better deal.

Chapter 4

Just because a new home and options are listed for a specific price does not mean that is what you have to pay. The following approach can be used to increase your chances of negotiating a better deal. Put down a deposit and select your lot, but make sure the deposit is refundable before you commit completely. Obtain the pricing for the home and all of the options that you selected. Tell them you would like a few days to think about it. This is a lot more than you were planning to spend, and you need to work out some figures.

Call the construction company salesperson in two days. Tell him/her that after you performed the calculations, your monthly payments were too high. You had set a limit based on a certain dollar amount you felt comfortable with. (Have a price in mind, maybe $22,000.00 less for a house that costs about $200,000.00. This price should be adjusted higher or lower depending on the price of the house.) Tell them you would like them to take $7,000.00 (or whatever reasonable figure you decided on) off the total cost of the house with the options you chose.

They may say that you can cut some of the options to lower the price. Say no, because that is why you are even considering spending more than your budget. (It's always easier to blame your spouse or significant other, say that he/she is not willing to purchase the house if they cannot get the house the way they want it.) If the developer tells you to add these things later, say once you move in the taxes and other expenses will continue to go up and you will not be able to afford to do it. Tell them you can understand if they cannot do this. No hard feelings. You will just have to keep looking. Ask them to get back to you with an answer as soon as possible.

It will usually take a few days for them to get back to you. They will try to offer you less of a discount. Stick to your guns and say you are already paying more than what you were planning to spend. They may need another day. The one thing to remember is that no matter what they offer you, you can always take their final offer. You can say someone in the family is going to help you out.

Helpful Hints / Comments:

Resales and New construction

Have your home inspected by an energy specialist. This can save you a great deal of money over the years by cutting down on your utility costs. Some utility companies offer this service free of charge.

There are companies that can provide a "snapshot" of your home. These companies use *infrared cameras* and other sophisticated gear. They can point out serious issues, such as leaks. If this is new construction, you may be able to ask the builder to make the repairs. Or you may decide to resolve them on your own. Either way, the longer you live in the home, the more you will save.

Also talk to neighbors. Do they know of any changes that are taking place now or in the future? Are they aware of any problems with the property you are looking to purchase?

Planting trees and shrubs in well-placed areas will shade your home and reduce wind exposure. This can save a great deal in utility costs. Trees that lose their leaves (also known as *deciduous* trees) are best when placed on the south and west side of the house. They shield your home from the sun during the summer months while allowing it to shine on your home during the winter. To deflect the wind, place evergreen trees (also known as *coniferous* trees) on the north and west side of the house. Trees are good for the environment. They grow by absorbing carbon dioxide, and they give off oxygen. This process cleans and cools the air around them.

Read Seller's Disclosure carefully.

Ask questions about the property, such as, "Have there ever been any problems related to the plumbing or electrical systems? Have any major repairs been done inside or outside of the home? Is there any build up of water on the grounds or in the house when it rains? Has anybody ever pointed out any problems or issues related to this home that have been corrected or are still outstanding?" These are just a few questions. People usually will not lie, but they often will not tell you unless you ask.

Point out all problems seen to the seller no matter how minor. This will give you ammunition to bid less than the asking price.

Plant trees and shrubs around the air conditioner, but do not block the unit. This will keep it in the shade, which will reduce the operating cost.

If you buy very efficient windows, you can reduce your costs by buying smaller air conditioning and heating systems. Look for windows that have a low *U-Value*, low SHGC (*solar heat gain coefficient*), and low air leakage rating. The lower the numbers the better the window. Also consider *Low-E glass*, which helps block most of the sun's damaging ultraviolet rays. This will help prevent your curtains, carpets, furniture, and wall coverings from fading due to sun exposure.

Check all walls inside for bowing or corners that may not be square.

Check comparable property around the area. Consult a realtor for a market analysis. Are the prices going up or down in recent sales.

Install storm windows over single pane glass windows.

Install an *insulated* ductwork system. It pays for itself if you live in the house for a while.

Ensure that you get a receipt for items that were permanently installed or used to maintain your property. You are often able to deduct these costs from the profit you make when you sell the house. (Check your local tax laws)

When purchasing a new or used property, you may need to hire an independent appraiser to obtain an accurate appraisal on the value of your property. The Web site below may help you locate an appraiser near you.

www.appraisalinstitute.org

Purchase toilets that have a shallow-trap. These use less water.

If you are building a fireplace, add an outside damper just below the firebox. It will save you money on your heating bills. To make the fireplace more efficient, add glass doors and a heat exchanger.

Use gaskets behind light switches and outlet plates on all exterior walls to prevent drafts.

Contact your local township or municipal building and ask to see the files that prospect usage for your surrounding area. Also ask to see the Federal Emergency Management Agency (FEMA) flood information maps and charts. As the property is being built, ask regularly to view the Inspection file. (This can be checked out for homes that are being resold. It may point out past fire or structural problems, etc.)

Selecting a white roof or lighter exterior colors will help keep your house cooler in the summer months.

Make sure, when purchasing, that appliances have high efficiency ratings, especially heating and air conditioning systems. They may cost more money, but will be less expensive to operate. Some items use a continuously burning pilot light. Look for *electronic ignition* systems instead, which turn on only when needed.

Step back and look at the house. See if anything appears to be out of place. Is the roof straight and neat or does it look as if it has been worked on. Do the walls appear to be plumb and flat? Look for items that may appear to be loose like siding, gutters, and fixtures.

When purchasing a resale, or new home, you should consider hiring a good home inspector. A home inspector can point out problems and issues the average homeowner would not see or know about. The Web site below may help you locate an inspector in your area.

www.ashi.com

New construction

Consider taking pictures regularly as the house is being built. This will help you if you want to remodel later. You will be aware of obstacles that may otherwise be hiding behind walls. Using a video camera would be even better. Take pictures/video of the outside of the structure and of all rooms from the inside. Make sure you get all walls, windows, and doors.

Install *house wrap* to keep the house more draft free.

Always know where the property line ends. Not just on paper. Go to your local township or municipal building and view the plans for the whole development. That will show you the sample *footprint* of the property, *contour line*, *elevation*, *grates*, *swale*, *easements*, *restrictions*, *basins*, who is responsible for surrounding maintenance, are you allowed to build, etc.

Most townships or municipal buildings hold bonds or escrows until new developments are 100% completed. If you are having any problems with your builder notify your local office.

Make sure all contractors you employ, for major renovations, are registered with your local township or municipal building.

If you have a choice between 2 x 6 framing and 2 x 4, choose the 2 x 6 if your region gets very cold or hot. It will allow for more insulation, which also helps cut down on noise.

Check with the builder to ensure that all items will be covered under warranty. What is the length of the warranty and how will they enforce it? Is there any cost to you?

Talk to the people at your local township or municipal building. They can provide you with a wealth of information. Just let them know you are building a new home and are open to their advice. This is a must. This alone will probably save you money and aggravation. Do this before making a final commitment.

Make sure all permits are filed. (This helps protect you in case of fire, and for structural safety, etc.)

Be prepared to live with construction vehicles on a daily basis, construction dirt, dust, no sidewalks, no trees, roads with only the first layer, etc., until the area is completed.

Chapter 5

Financial Pointers

Banking

Banking, that is a good one. That used to be where you put your money in a safe place and they actual paid you a good interest rate for it. Today you give them your money, they give you a minimal interest rate, and they charge you all kinds of fees. By the time you are finished, you end up owing the bank money. There are still a few good banks out there but most of them are smaller banks. The smaller banks offer many of the services for free that the larger banks charge for. A nice thing about the smaller banks is that they know who you are. Internet banks often have very limited services, but they usually pay a decent interest rate. Many of them do not have a minimum balance. You access these accounts over the Internet. You usually have to transfer funds electronically from one bank account to another. It takes about 24 hours to do this. I think they are great when you have the savings account connected to your checking account. This way your money can sit in the savings account collecting interest until you need it.

One good way to save money is to consolidate all of your accounts into one bank, so you can try to avoid paying fees. Some banks waive many of their fees if your total deposits exceed a certain amount. Do not, however, put more than $100,000.00 in any one bank, because that is the highest amount that the money is federally insured for.

How about ATM (*automated teller machine*) fees? Did you know you are charged twice when you use a foreign ATM (another bank's ATM other than the bank that holds your account)? Not only does your bank charge you, but the other bank may also charge you. Try to avoid using foreign ATMs.

Many of us use the ATM a few times a week to get cash. We take out just a little each time. Some banks charge fees for having too many ATM transactions within the same month. So take out more money when you go, and cut back on the number of trips to the ATM to save on these fees.

Buying Insurance

When deciding to buy insurance, look for an independent insurance *broker*. They can tell you which companies offer the cheapest rates. Insurance brokers do not work for the insurance companies. They are completely independent and receive their commission from the company to which they refer you.

You could also shop on the Internet. Some sites will send your information to multiple insurance carriers at once. You will receive quotes back from companies interested in doing business with you. One problem you may run into, however, is that not all insurance carriers participate with these sites. The Internet is a great tool, but when it comes to insurance, I would rather speak to a live person. If you are shopping for regular term life insurance, the Internet is fine.

If you do not use a broker, shop around by phone. Find numbers in your local phone book in the insurance section. (Keep in mind that the local phone book may not have all available insurance companies listed.) If you are shopping to replace an existing policy, make sure you have a copy of your present insurance policy in front of you so that you have all of the information readily available. Call the companies one by one. Tell them you are shopping around for insurance and will select the least expensive insurance company that matches your existing policy and features. No matter what service you choose, I still think it is best to have a permanent local agent, even if it costs you a few dollars more. Always consult your existing insurance company if you are considering leaving them for a better price elsewhere. Sometimes they can adjust your premium. You may reconsider leaving if the price difference is minimal and you have had a good relationship with your present agent and company.

Whichever insurance company you select, ask them to send you the information in writing before you cancel your existing policy. Tell the new agent you want them to perform the background check before you cancel your existing policy. This way you can be assured that they will not change the pricing structure or cancel you for one reason or another. Once the new company has accepted you, and you are comfortable with the rates, cancel your other policy, effective to the date you started with the new company. Let them know you want to be reimbursed to the day you started your new insurance. Ask the new company to send proof of insurance and to send a cancellation notice to your old company. You should also notify your existing agent of the cancellation.

Be careful when comparing prices. Some companies offer policies based on a 6-month term, while others offer a one-year term. You should compare your insurance rate annually because rates are constantly changing, especially automobile insurance.

Make sure your insurance agent is aware of all items in your home or car that may qualify you for an insurance discount.

Home	Car
Premise burglar alarm	Car alarm
Fire alarm	Engine demobilizer
New home discount	Starter demobilizer
Newly built property	Accident or claim free
Claim free	Driver's education
If over 55 or 60	Good student discount
Close to fire station	Good driving record
Sprinkler system	Low mileage
Close to fire hydrant	Teenager away at college
Longevity with company	*Airbags*
	Window etching
	Lo Jack
	Antilock brake system (ABS)

Another way to save money on insurance is to combine multiple policies, such as home and car insurance. Most companies give you discounts on combined policies.

Many people select a low deductible on their policies, which increases the cost. This may not be the most cost-effective choice. For example, let us say your car insurance deductible is $100.00 and you are involved in a minor fender bender. The repairs cost $500.00. Most people would rather pay the $500.00 out of their own pocket and avoid filing a claim with the insurance company. When you file a claim, it becomes part of your permanent record and could lead to a surcharge in the future. If this scenario describes you, then by all means, raise your deductible to $200.00 or more and start saving money immediately.

Make sure your policy covers everything you have, at the limit you require. Many times we choose the deluxe policy only to discover that it does not cover everything we have. Or the items that are covered are only insured up to $500.00, and you have $7,000.00 worth of them. Some things you should be concerned about include: Jewelry, guns, silverware, furs, collectibles, computers, flood insurance, water or sewer backup coverage, liability insurance (if you have a trampoline or swimming pool), etc. Share your lifestyle with your agent. Ask the agent if there is some type of coverage you should have, that you do not have. However, do not over-insure for items that are not worth the value. If your vehicle is over ten years old, you may want to consider removing collision and comprehensive coverage from your policy.

Here are a few other things to consider. If your license was *revoked, suspended,* or you just have many traffic points from violations, you will probably not be able to obtain an inexpensive automobile insurance rate. In today's world companies are also looking at your credit history to determine if you qualify for insurance. In fact, many companies may not even want your business because they consider you a high risk due to poor credit history or driving record. You will need to get your driving and credit records straightened out first. You must maintain a good driving record for at least two or three years before you can qualify for lower rates. In most states you need to have insurance before you can get your driver's license back once it has been revoked.

Notify your insurance company immediately if you move or change your vehicle. This can result in a major change in your premium and/or coverage. If you are considering buying insurance outside of your local area, be sure the company has a claim office near you.

I cannot take credit for this idea, but I thought it was very important. A friend of mine who is in the insurance business mentioned this when I told him about writing this book. He indicated that many people who rent property do not have insurance on the contents of their home because they feel that they are covered by the owner's property insurance. In most cases this is not true. If there were a fire at the property, you would not receive any compensation for your lost belongings.

Credit Cards

Some of us like to use credit cards, others do not. Credit cards can be very powerful tools in helping you financially over the course of your life. They can also really hurt you if you do not manage them properly. I believe credit cards are very good as long as you can control your spending habits. If you cannot do that, then you should cut up and throw away your credit cards.

There are many credit cards available today. Some companies charge low interest rates, while others charge such steep fees that they may as well just take your wallet each month. If you have credit cards like this, you should consider consolidating all of your balances into a loan or another credit card with a much lower interest rate. In some cases you can renegotiate a lower interest rate with your existing credit card company. If they are not willing to do this, let them know you will transfer your total balance to another credit card.

Look for one of the new cards that offer a free balance transfer. Many also offer one to six months interest-free. You may look for another card that offers these same benefits when the interest-free period runs out, and then switch cards again. You do need to be concerned about how many credit cards you have in your name. Sometimes you may not qualify for more credit if you already have too many credit cards. Close out accounts that are no longer being used. Some cards charge an annual fee, some do not. Some pay you cash back when you use them, and others give you points toward the purchase of certain items. You should consider all of the features before you make a commitment. There are Web sites that can provide information on many of the credit card companies. (Be careful because they do not have a complete list of all of the companies, so you may not get an accurate comparison in all instances.)

I think credit cards are important to have. They can actually help protect the consumer when making purchases and if disputes arise related to the product. They also make it convenient to order items by mail or over the Internet. Sometimes they help with record keeping. I would never make a large purchase without my credit card. I feel better knowing that if I have a problem, I have a way to resolve it. I have had many experiences where products that I had purchased were either defective or I changed my mind after I had the product home. Sometimes companies are not quick to accept returns. My credit card company was able to help me resolve all of those issues. I have learned not all credit card companies are the same. Some handle customer service issues much better than others. When I have encountered difficulties over the years, the other credit card companies did not have the same resolution rate as my Discover Card. I asked them why my Discover Card Company could resolve these issues and they could not. I was told that they do not have to follow the same laws.

I personally like to use the Discover card because it has no annual fee and it pays me cash back as I charge. I only charge items when I have the money to pay the bill. I charge things throughout the month and allow my money to sit in a savings account earning interest. At the end of the month I pay the balance off completely. Today you can charge just about anything. I charge my groceries, gas, insurance, trash pick-up, cable TV bill, Internet service provider, and other routine purchases on that card. The cash back payment can add up to a couple of nice presents for you at the end of the year.

If you think this is good, it gets better. Many grocery stores allow you to take up to thirty dollars in cash when you pay for your purchases with the credit card. The amount is added to your bill. They treat the transaction as a credit card purchase, not a cash advance. There are no transaction fees. They are actually giving you money interest free. They even count that money when computing your cash back payment amount. It is also convenient because you do not have to make a special trip to the ATM.

If you use your credit card routinely, you can build very good credit, assuming you pay your bills on time. The higher your credit limit, the easier it will be to get new credit cards or loans. It also helps you when applying for a new job, insurance, etc. Good credit is becoming very important. Many companies today look at your credit history before they accept you. Credit cards offer many other benefits when you use them to pay for purchases. Some of the more common benefits, included free of charge, are flight insurance, car rental insurance, extended warranties on purchases, and travel accident insurance.

Helpful Hints / Comments:

Many banks no longer provide free checks. Consider purchasing them from a check printing company. You can save 40% or more over bank prices. Look for ads in your local Sunday paper or on the Internet.

Take your copy of your signed receipt. Do not leave it in the store where someone else may pick it up. The person would then have your credit card account number and a copy of your signature.

If you file for bankruptcy, companies, creditors, and collection agencies are no longer allowed to contact you.

Never take out a loan that uses your residence as collateral unless you can easily make the payments.

If an item breaks after the manufacturer's warranty has expired, you may still have an extended warranty through the credit card company. Many credit card companies offer extended warranties but you may need to register the item with them. Some cards offer insurance that covers you in the event you accidentally damage the item, or if it is stolen within a few months of your purchase date.

If a collection agency approaches you for immediate payment, do not write them a post dated check if you do not have the funds in your account. They are not allowed to ask you to do that. It is considered illegal. The bank could cash it and you would be penalized for bouncing the check. If you choose to do this on your own, you can write on it in big red letters "post dated check" and sign the check in red ink.

Many credit card companies offer you a grace period. This is the period between the time of the purchase and the day they begin to charge interest on that purchase. Some companies actually start charging interest as early as the day after the charge is applied. They usually do this when people carry a balance from month to month.

If your credit card is stolen, you have limited liability as long as you report the theft as soon as you become aware of it.

If you find yourself constantly tempted or are an impulsive buyer, leave the credit card at home or dispose of it.

If you pay only the minimum balance each month, you will continue to get deeper and deeper into debt. Many people do not realize they are in over their heads until it is too late. Paying those ridiculous interest rates each month is like throwing your money away. Remember, if you cannot control your spending, cut the cards up and throw them away. You could get a debit card. A debit card takes the money from your checking account at the time of purchase. If you do not have any money in the account, you will not be able to use your card.

You should only spend money when you have it to spend. If you feel you cannot do it yourself, there are people and organizations that can help you. Below are just a few Web sites. Most of these organizations represent you and are able to work out deals with your creditors so you can get out of debt. Some of the sites do charge a fee. Most people can be debt free in three to five years. It is a great feeling once you have control of your finances. Whatever you do, do not open another credit card account and do not take out a loan if you cannot afford the payment. That will only prolong the time it takes to realize how bad things really are. In fact, it will just get you deeper in debt. Make that first move today.

www.DebtSynergy.com   www.nfcc.org
www.Amerix.com   myvesta.org
www.GoDebtFree.com
www.DebtConsolidationPros.com
www.Non-Profit-Credit-Counseling.org

When applying for credit cards or loans, do not mention previous loans if you do not have to. Sometimes these can have a negative impact on your application, even if they have been repaid.

Do not fall for the old trick where the credit card company lets you skip a month's payment. Yes, they are being so nice but they are probably adding the finance charges to your future bill, which is putting you deeper in debt.

If you are late making payments, do not use marital problems as an excuse. This will raise red flags because they will think you may soon be getting divorced. This may cause them to start collection procedures, when they may have been willing to work with you originally. Some acceptable excuses are medical bills, job loss, health related issues, etc.

Do not use a credit card to make late or partial payments on another credit card bill. If you cannot meet your financial obligations contact the credit card company as soon as possible to work out a payment plan. (Most companies are willing to work with you.) Sometimes you can ask the credit card company to suspend your card for a period of time, or until you pay off the debt. This may keep them from marking your credit report negatively. Sometimes you may even be able to get the card back once you are paid up.

Below are lists of Web sites that will help you with credit card related information. These sites have information on choosing some of the best credit cards, how to consolidate credit card debt, watching out for credit card traps, regulations, what to do if you are overextended, first time credit card holders, plus many other interesting facts. If you look through these sites, you will find many good links to other sites. There are many other sites out there; you just need to look for them. The sites were all working as of the day this chapter was written.

www.nelliemae.com/managingmoney/cc_tips.html
www.occ.treas.gov   www.truthaboutcredit.org
www.bankrate.com   www.cardweb.com

Most companies or creditors will not take you to court if the debt is small. The cost and time involved is not worth it for them, but they will affect your credit report in a negative way.

Companies are usually willing to settle for a smaller percentage of the debt in order to resolve the problem. Request in return that they mark your account closed and paid in full. They will often do this if you have a very good reason for the debt. They would rather do this than turn it over to a collection agency. They may have to pay the collection company as much as 50% for any money they collect.

If you have poor credit or are trying to re-establish new credit after bankruptcy, try the following. Look for banks that are competing for business and apply to them. The worst that can happen is they will turn you down. If married you can always have your wife apply under her maiden name. You could also flash an old credit card at a local department store that gives credit on the spot and start charging immediately. You may start out with a small credit limit, but this will help you rebuild your credit. Just make sure you pay your bills on time.

Think twice before buying a sporty, high powered or expensive vehicle. It may have a large impact on your auto insurance rates. In some areas you may even have trouble getting insurance coverage.

Below are a few Web sites that will help you with insurance quotes and information. The Web sites are usually in lower case letters, but I like to capitalize the first letter in the name or word because it makes it easier to remember that way.

www.InsWeb.com   www.naic.org
www.QuoteSmith.com   www.4ezquotes.com
www.netquote.com

Chapter 6

Sale Items

We often buy items when they are not on sale. Many times we may not have the patience, or luxury, to wait until an item goes on sale. Follow these easy steps to take advantage of sale prices more often at your favorite store. Buy the item you want and keep the receipt and packing material that came with the item. Each week check the Sunday newspaper, and other ads, watching for that item. If you find the item on sale at the store where you purchased it, take the ad and your receipt and return to the store. Go to the customer service desk and simply say the item has gone on sale since you bought it and you would like a refund on the difference. (Make sure the ad has the store name and dates of the sale.) Most stores are willing to refund the difference as long as it is within fourteen to thirty days from the date of purchase.

If it has been more than thirty days but less than ninety since the purchase, I would still try to obtain the refund. If they refuse to do it, tell the customer service person that you could just repurchase the item and then return it on the old receipt. Tell them you would prefer to make it easier on them if he/she would just take care of the credit. (Some stores may offer you an in-store credit for the difference.) If they still refuse to refund the difference, go and purchase the same item at the sale price. You can now return the new item under the old receipt. Most stores allow you to return items within ninety days as long as you have the receipt. If the item is from the same store and you have the receipt and it is in the original packing, most companies will take the item back even after ninety days.

You could even return to the store with an item and say that you just received it as a gift and do not have receipt. In this case they will usually give you a store credit based on the lowest price at which the item was sold in the past six months. This is a good option if you bought something and changed your mind about it many months later, as long as you never used it. Sometimes you could run into a problem if the item is no longer being sold in that store.

If the item happens to be on sale at a different store, cut out the ad and return to the original store with your receipt. Go to the customer service desk and simply say that the item has gone on sale at another store and you would like them to refund the difference. If they refuse, tell them you will buy the item at their competitor's store and then you will come back and return their item to them. Most of the time they will take care of you. They will sometimes do so even after thirty days.

In the past four paragraphs, I have given you examples on how to deal with customer service personnel. If they are not willing to satisfy your request, ask for the store manager, not a department manager. What you need to remember is that most of the people at the customer service desk must follow store procedures. In order to do something different they need management approval. It is not such a bad thing if you look at it from their side. If you stand by one of these customer service desks, you would be surprised at how many people just walk away when they are denied a refund or exchange, rather than assert themselves. Some stores do give their staff a little more freedom to override policy.

I have run into situations where a business says that they do match prices, yet they will not compete with stores that are located more than so many miles from their store. In these cases, you should ask to speak with the store manager. If the store manager will not help you, call their corporate headquarters. Remember to ask for a further discount because you now have to make a second trip to the store to get your refund, plus the aggravation that you received in the store on your first trip.

I know that some people may not have time to waste on small ticket priced items, but think of it as being paid for your time. Over the course of a year, it adds up and you can use the money for other things. Remember that for most of us who work, if you can save ten dollars, it is equivalent to being paid at least $12.50, by your employer, because you must pay taxes on your wages.

The best thing about reading this chapter is that you can shop at a store near your home and still be sure you are getting the best price.

Helpful Hints / Comments:

If you return an item to the store, make sure you get your receipt back if there are other items on it. You may need it later for another reason.

If you purchase a product and it breaks within the first 90 days, return it to the store rather than go through the hassles of the warranty procedures.

Sometimes businesses purposely change the model number by one digit to throw you off when comparing prices. Some manufacturers actually make the same identical product for different stores and give them a slightly different model number. (This protects the store from having to match prices on the product because they are the only one that carries that specific model number.)

Check and see if the manufacturer or store is offering any rebates on the item that you purchased. You can often find the rebates by the customer service desk, or by the front of the store near the cash registers. Always ask the store to print you a duplicate receipt for the rebate. Be sure to keep the original because most stores will not accept copies for returns or a price match.

Chapter 7

Dealing with Funerals

This is one subject I really did not want to write about, but too many people are taken when a loved one passes on. We are grieving and under emotional duress, yet we need to make the funeral arrangements almost immediately. When these situations arise, we are often not thinking clearly, yet we have to make some major and costly decisions.

We are faced with many decisions. Where should I have the funeral? How much should I spend? Whom do I need to notify? What were the person's last requests? Did the deceased want their body, or any part of their body, donated to science? What is the family going to think about the funeral? This all creates a lot of stress and most of us want to just put it behind us so we can grieve.

I think it is best if some, or most, of the decisions could be made in advance. I know it is a subject that we do not like to talk about, but you should ask your loved ones what they would like before the time arises. Have them write down what they would like. Keep the paperwork in a safe place where you can get to it easily. When the time comes, you will not have to wonder if you are doing the right thing. An increasing number of people are planning their own funerals, designating their funeral preferences, and sometimes even paying for them in advance (pre-paid). They see funeral planning as an extension of their will and estate planning.

I recommend that you take someone close to you along when you go to make arrangements. Make sure all of the costs are broken down the same way so you can easily compare pricing. And, as callous as it may sound, how much is it all going to cost? We all want the best for our loved ones but we do not want to go broke or be in debt because of it. Believe me, your loved one would not want you to put yourself into hardship over their funeral. Do not let family members pressure you into things you do not feel comfortable with. Many times this tends to be the focus of a lot of our stress.

All families are different, and not everyone wants the same type of funeral. The funeral itself is influenced by religion, culture, cost, and personal preference. These factors help determine whether the funeral will be elaborate or simple, public or private, religious or secular, and where it will be held. They also influence whether or not the body will be present at the funeral, if there will be a viewing or visitation, and if so, whether the *casket* will be open or closed, and whether the remains will be buried or cremated. Among the choices you will need to make are whether you want a basic funeral (*traditional*, *direct burial*, *direct cremation*), or something in between.

People often select a funeral home or cemetery because it is close to home, they have used it before, or someone you trust has recommended it. However, people who limit their search to just one funeral home may risk paying more than is necessary for the funeral or narrowing their choice of goods and services. Begin by going to, or calling, at least two funeral providers away from your home area and let them quote you their best prices. Compare the casket prices with some of the companies listed at the end of this chapter, or with other providers. If prices are lower than the funeral provider quoted you, show the funeral provider the prices others are willing to give you. Then ask them to match it or to lower his/her price. You are now armed with the information to take to the funeral provider that you really would like to do business with. If they are not willing to lower the price for a casket, order it directly from another source, and have it shipped to your funeral provider's address. When comparing these prices, be sure to include the cost of shipping and handling. It can be shipped in one to two days.

If you visit a funeral home in person, the funeral provider is required by law to give you a general price list itemizing the cost of the items and services the home offers. If the general price list does not include specific prices of caskets or outer burial containers, the law requires the funeral director to show you the price lists for those items before showing you the items. Sometimes it is more convenient and less stressful to "price shop" funeral homes by telephone. The Funeral Rule requires funeral directors to provide price information over the phone to any caller who asks for it.

When comparing prices, be sure to consider the total cost of all of the items together, not only the costs of single items. Every funeral home should provide price lists that include all of the items essential for the different types of arrangements it offers. Many funeral homes offer funeral packages that may cost less than purchasing individual items or services. Offering funeral packages is permitted by law, as long as an itemized price list is also provided. Only by using the price lists can you accurately compare total costs.

People, who normally haggle for the best price on a new car, usually feel uncomfortable comparing prices or negotiating the details and cost of a funeral. Compounding this discomfort is the fact that some people "overspend" on a funeral, or burial, because they think of it as a reflection of their feelings for the deceased. Do not let anyone take advantage of you because you are grieving.

A traditional funeral, including a casket and *vault*, costs about $4,500.00, although "extras" like flowers, obituary notices, acknowledgment cards, or limousines can add thousands of dollars to the bottom line. Many funerals run well over $10,000.00. This price does not include the cemetery costs, which usually start at $2,500.00 and up. They are expensive, but you can fight back by comparing prices and negotiating a better contract.

Funeral costs normally include the following items:

1. Basic services fee for the funeral director and staff

The Funeral Rule allows funeral providers to charge a basic services fee that customers cannot decline to pay. The basic services fee includes services that are common to all funerals, regardless of any specific arrangements. These include funeral planning, securing the necessary permits and copies of death certificates, preparing the notices, sheltering the remains, and coordinating the arrangements with the cemetery, crematory, or other third parties. The fee does not include charges for optional services or merchandise.

2. Charges for other services and merchandise
These are costs for optional goods and services such as transporting the remains, *embalming* and other preparation, use of the funeral home for the viewing, ceremony or *memorial service,* use of equipment and staff for a *graveside service*, use of a hearse or limousine, a casket, outer burial container or alternate container, and *cremation* or *interment.*

3. Cash advances
These are fees charged by the funeral home for goods and services it buys from outside vendors on your behalf, including flowers, obituary notices, pallbearers, officiating clergy, and organists/ soloists. Some funeral providers charge you their cost for the items they buy on your behalf. Others add a service fee to their cost. The Funeral Rule requires those who charge an extra fee to disclose that fact in writing, although it does not require them to specify the amount of their *markup*. The Funeral Rule also requires funeral providers to tell you if there are refunds, discounts, or rebates from the supplier on any cash advanced item.

The funeral provider must give you an itemized statement showing the total cost of the funeral goods and services you have selected when making the arrangements. This statement also must disclose any legal, cemetery or crematory requirements when you purchase any specific funeral goods or services. If the funeral provider does not know the cost of the cash advance items at the time, he or she is required to give you a written "good faith estimate." The Funeral Rule does not require any specific format for this information. Funeral providers may include it in any document they give you at the end of your discussion concerning funeral arrangements.

Some of the more common products and services include embalming, caskets, cemetery plots, burial vaults, or *grave liners*. Many funeral homes require embalming if you are planning a viewing or visitation. However, embalming generally is not necessary or legally required if the body is buried or cremated shortly after death. Eliminating this service can save you hundreds of dollars.

Under the Funeral Rule, a funeral provider:

- May not provide embalming services without permission.
- May not falsely state that embalming is required by law.
- Must disclose in writing that embalming is not required by law, except in certain special cases.
- May not charge a fee for unauthorized embalming unless embalming is required by state law.
- Must disclose in writing that you usually have the right to choose a *disposition*, such as direct cremation or immediate burial that does not require embalming if you do not want this service.
- Must disclose in writing that some funeral arrangements, such as a funeral with viewing, may make embalming a practical necessity and, if so, a required purchase.

Caskets are usually the single most expensive item you will buy for a funeral. Caskets vary widely in style and price, and are sold primarily for their visual appeal. Typically, they are constructed of metal, wood, fiberboard, fiberglass, or plastic. Although an average casket costs slightly more than $2,000.00, some mahogany, bronze, or copper caskets can sell for as much as $10,000.00.

When you visit a funeral home or showroom to shop for a casket, the Funeral Rule requires the funeral director to show you a list of caskets the company sells, with descriptions and prices, before showing you the caskets. Studies show that the average casket shopper buys one of the first three models shown, generally the middle-priced of the three. It is in the seller's best interest to start out by showing you higher-end models. If you have not seen some of the lower-priced models on the price list, ask to see them - but do not be surprised if they are not prominently displayed, or not on display at all.

Traditionally, caskets have been sold only by funeral homes. But with increasing frequency, showrooms and Web sites operated by "third-party" dealers are selling caskets. You can buy a casket from one of these dealers and have it shipped directly to the funeral home. The Funeral Rule requires funeral homes to agree to use a casket you bought elsewhere, and does not allow them to charge you an additional fee for using it.

No matter where or when you are buying a casket, it is important to remember that its purpose is to provide a dignified way to move the body before burial or cremation. No casket, regardless of its qualities or cost, will preserve a body forever. The Funeral Rule forbids claims that these features help preserve the remains indefinitely, because they do not.

Most metal caskets are made from rolled steel of varying gauges - the lower the gauge, the thicker the steel. Some metal caskets come with a warranty for longevity. Wooden caskets generally are not *gasketed* and do not have a warranty for longevity. They can be hardwood like cherry, mahogany, oak, walnut, or softwood like pine. Pine caskets are less expensive, but funeral homes rarely display them. Manufacturers of both wooden and metal caskets usually warrant workmanship and materials.

Many families that opt to have their loved ones cremated rent a casket from the funeral home for the visitation and funeral, eliminating the cost of buying a casket. If you opt for visitation and cremation, ask about the rental option. For those who choose a direct cremation without a viewing or other ceremony where the body is present, the funeral provider must offer an inexpensive unfinished wood box or alternative non-metal container - pressboard, cardboard or canvas - that is cremated with the body.

Under the Funeral Rule, funeral directors who offer direct cremations:

- May not tell you that state or local laws require a casket for direct cremations, because none do.
- Must disclose in writing your right to buy an unfinished wood box or an *alternative container* for a direct cremation.
- Must make an unfinished wood box or other alternative container available for direct cremations.

Burial vaults or grave liners, also known as burial containers, are commonly used in traditional funerals. The vault or liner is placed in the ground before burial, and the casket is lowered into it at burial. The purpose is to prevent the ground from caving in as the casket deteriorates over time. A grave liner is made of reinforced concrete and will satisfy any cemetery requirement. Grave liners cover only the top and sides of the casket. A burial vault is more substantial and expensive than a grave liner. It surrounds the casket in concrete, or another material, and may be sold with a warranty of protective strength.

State laws do not require a vault or liner, and funeral providers may not tell you otherwise. Many cemeteries, however, require some type of outer burial container to prevent the *grave* from sinking in the future. Neither grave liners nor burial vaults are designed to prevent the eventual decomposition of human remains.

Before showing you any outer burial containers, a funeral provider is required to give you a list of prices and descriptions. It may be less expensive to buy an outer burial container from a third-party dealer than from a funeral home or cemetery. Compare prices from several sources before selecting a model.

When you are purchasing a cemetery plot, consider the location of the cemetery and whether it meets your family's religious requirements. Other considerations include what, if any, restrictions the cemetery places on burial vaults purchased elsewhere, the type of monuments or memorials it allows, and whether flowers or other remembrances may be placed on graves.

Cost is also a consideration. Cemetery plots can be expensive, especially in metropolitan areas. Note that there are charges to open a grave for interment and additional charges to fill it in. They also charge you extra on weekends. Perpetual care on a cemetery plot sometimes is included in the purchase price, but it is important to clarify that point before you purchase the site or service. If it is not included, look for a separate *endowment care* fee for maintenance and grounds keeping.

If you plan to bury your loved one's cremated remains in a *mausoleum* or *columbarium*, you can expect to purchase a *crypt* and pay opening and closing fees, as well as charges for endowment care and other services.

The FTC's Funeral Rule does not cover cemeteries and mausoleums unless they sell both funeral goods and funeral services, so be cautious in making your purchase to ensure that you receive all pertinent pricing and other information, and that you're being dealt with fairly.

Helpful Hints / Comments:

It is very important to keep notes about your conversations because you are probably not thinking clearly.

Have the funeral provider write down all information in detail. Ask them to be very specific about each item, option, or service.

Following these steps will help you in planning for a funeral.
1. Shop around in advance. Compare prices from at least three funeral homes. **Remember that you can supply your own casket or *urn*.**

2. Ask for a price list. The law requires funeral homes to give you written price lists for products and services.
3. Resist pressure to buy goods and services you do not really want or need.
4. Avoid emotional overspending. It is not necessary to have the fanciest casket or the most elaborate funeral to properly honor a loved one.
5. Recognize your rights. Laws regarding funerals and burials vary from state to state. It is a smart move to know which goods or services the law requires you to purchase and which are optional.
6. Apply your new skills that you learned in previous chapters to get the lowest price. You can cut costs by limiting the viewing to one day or one hour before the funeral, and by dressing your loved one in a favorite outfit instead of costly burial clothing.

Remember, if you plan ahead, you will be able to comparison shop without time constraints; this creates an opportunity for family discussion, and lifts some of the burden from your family.

You can open a Pre Arranged Burial Account. The purpose of this account is to set aside funds for burial expenses. The account is titled in the individual's name with a funeral home as the trustee. This is an easy method to set money aside and no lawyers are needed. Just open a savings account in a federally insured bank and deposit the amount needed to cover the cost of the funeral.

Most funeral providers are professionals who strive to serve their clients' needs and best interests. But some are not. They may take advantage of their clients by inflating prices, overcharging, double charging, or stressing unnecessary services. There's a federal law that makes it easier for you to choose only those goods and services you want or need, and to pay only for those you select, whether you are making arrangements pre-need or at need.

The Funeral Rule, enforced by the Federal Trade Commission, requires funeral directors to give you itemized prices in person and, if you ask, **over the phone**. The Rule also requires funeral directors to give you other information about their goods and services. For example, if you ask about funeral arrangements in person, the funeral home must give you a written price list to keep, that shows the goods and services the home offers. If you want to buy a casket or outer burial container, the funeral provider must show you descriptions of the available selections and the prices before actually showing you the caskets.

Many funeral providers offer various "packages" of commonly selected goods and services that make up a funeral. However, when you arrange for a funeral, you have the right to buy individual goods and services. That is, you do not have to accept a package that may include items you do not want.

According to the Funeral Rule:
- You have the right to choose the funeral goods and services you want (with some exceptions). The funeral provider must state this right in writing on the general price list.
- If state or local law requires you to buy any particular item, the funeral provider must disclose it on the price list, with a reference to the specific law.
- The funeral provider may not refuse, or charge a fee, to handle a casket you bought elsewhere.
- A funeral provider that offers cremations must make alternative containers available.

Many people do not realize that they are not legally required to use a funeral home to plan and conduct a funeral. However, because they have little experience with the many details and legal requirements involved, and may be emotionally distraught when it is time to make the plans, many people find the services of a professional funeral home to be a comfort.

Many funeral providers are owned by large corporations. They keep their original name so that people do not know. Ask them if they are locally owned if this is important to you.

Make copies of the following information and check with several funeral homes to compare costs. This is a list of things you need to discuss with the funeral provider. Get a total price first and then ask them to provide a breakdown and description for each item. This will make it easier to shop around.

"Simple" disposition of the remains:

Immediate burial	$_____
Immediate cremation	$_____
If the cremation process is extra, how much is it?	$_____
Donation of the body to a medical school or hospital	$_____
Total	$_____

"Traditional," full-service burial or cremation:

Basic services fee for the funeral director and staff	$_____
Pickup of body	$_____
Embalming	$_____
Other preparation of body	$_____
Least expensive casket. Description, including model number _____	$_____
Outer Burial Container (vault) Description	$_____
_____	
Visitation/viewing - staff and facilities	$_____
Funeral or memorial service - staff and facilities	$_____
Graveside service, including staff and equipment	$_____
Hearse	$_____
Other vehicles	$_____
Total	$_____

Other Services:

Forwarding body to another funeral home	$_____
Receiving body from another funeral home	$_____

Cemetery/Mausoleum Costs:

Cost of lot or crypt (if you don't already own one)	$_____
Perpetual care	$_____
Opening and closing the grave or crypt	$_____
Grave liner, if required	$_____
Marker/monument (including setup)	$_____

Protect your family and loved ones by creating a Living Will. This will protect your advanced decision, to either be kept on artificial life support or not.

If you need to fly to another state to attend a relative's funeral, the airline will make every effort to get you on the next available flight. In most cases, they will even overlook fare restrictions to provide you with cheaper rates. You will need to prove your relationship with the deceased and provide proof of death.

Below are Web sites that provide information on caskets and other funeral related material. In some states, the Web sites can coordinate the entire funeral, but they must hold a license in your state. Most of the places can ship caskets to the funeral provider within twenty-four hours. The savings can be from forty to fifty percent. There are many other sites out there, you just need to explore. The sites were all working as of the day this chapter was being written.

www.TheCasketStores.com
800-350-4758

www.FuneralDepot.com
800-318-8707

www.CasketGallery.com
888-782-2753

www.DirectCasket.com
East Coast 800-732-2753
West Coast 800-772-2753

Funeral Service Foundation (FSF)
13625 Bishop's Drive
Brookfield, WI 53005
877-402-5900
FSF is a nonprofit foundation providing resources through charitable gifts and grants for educating the public about funeral service, professional development, and support of funeral service and allied professions.
www.funeralservicefoundation.org

National Funeral Directors Association (NFDA)
13625 Bishop's Drive
Brookfield, WI 53005
800-228-6332

NFDA is the largest educational and professional association of funeral directors. www.nfda.org

National Funeral Directors and Morticians Association
3951 Snapfinger Parkway
Suite 570
Decatur, GA 30035
800-434-0958
NFDMA is a national association primarily of African-American funeral providers.   www.nfdma.com

Selected Independent Funeral Homes
5 Revere Drive, Suite 340
Northbrook, IL 60062
800-323-4219
Selected Independent Funeral Homes is a nonprofit international association of funeral firms that have agreed to comply with its Code of Good Funeral Practice. www.selectedfuneralhomes.org

Funeral Service Consumer Assistance Program
PO Box 486
Elm Grove, WI 53122-0486
800-662-7666
FSCAP is a nonprofit consumer assistance service that helps consumers gain better understanding of funeral service issues and resolve funeral-related concerns. They offer free information and resources including materials focusing on understanding grief. www.nfda.org

Funeral Consumers Alliance (FCA)
P.O. Box 10
Hinesburg, Vermont 05461
800-765-0107
802-482-3437
FCA is a nonprofit, educational organization that supports increased funeral consumer protection. www.funerals.org

If you have a problem concerning funeral matters, it is best to try to resolve it first with the funeral director. If you are dissatisfied, the Funeral Consumers Alliance may be able to advise you on how to resolve your issue. You also can contact your state or local consumer protection agencies listed in your telephone book, or the Funeral Service Consumer Assistance Program.

You can file a complaint with the Federal Trade Commission (FTC) by contacting the Consumer Response Center by phone, toll-free, at 877-FTC-HELP (382-4357); TDD: 866-653-4261; by mail: Consumer Response Center, Federal Trade Commission, 600 Pennsylvania Avenue, NW, Washington, DC 20580; or on the Internet at www.ftc.gov, using the online complaint form. Although the Commission cannot resolve individual problems for consumers, it can act against a company if it sees a pattern of possible law violations.

AARP
601 E St., NW
Washington, DC 20049
Phone: 800-424-3410
AARP is a nonprofit, nonpartisan organization dedicated to helping older Americans achieve lives of independence, dignity, and purpose. There is funeral-related information posted on the AARP Web site.   www.aarp.org

Jewish Funeral Directors of America Seaport Landing
150 Lynnway
Suite 506
Lynn, MA 01902
(781) 477-9300
JFDA is an international association of funeral homes serving the Jewish community. www.jfda.org

International Order of the Golden Rule
13523 Lakefront Drive
St. Louis, MO 63045
800-637-8030
OGR is an association of 1,100 independently owned and operated funeral homes. www.ogr.org

Cremation Association of North America
401 North Michigan Avenue
Chicago, IL 60611
(312) 644-6610
CANA is an association of crematories, cemeteries, and funeral homes that offer cremation. CANA offers a series of consumer brochures explaining cremation and the many options that are available to those who choose cremation. www.cremationassociation.org

International Cemetery and Funeral Association
1895 Preston White Drive
Suite 220
Reston, VA 20191
800-645-7700
ICFA is a nonprofit association of cemeteries, funeral homes, crematories, and monument retailers that offers informal mediation of consumer complaints through its Cemetery Consumer Service Council. Its Website provides information and advice under "Consumer Resources."   www.icfa.org

Funeral Homes Directory
This last site has a comprehensive directory of funeral homes and other services. You will also find links to funeral homes, florists, and other services necessary to planning a funeral. www.funeralhomesdirectory.com

References

Federal Trade Commission

Chapter 8

Other Ways to Save

There are many ways to save money. The key to doing this is to first identify what you spend your money on. Start by creating a detailed list of everything you buy over the course of a month. This should include all purchases no matter how inexpensive. Once you create this list, review each item and determine if any were unnecessary and which ones you cannot do without. Now that you know what you spend each month, how much do you earn? Add up all of your income, and then subtract your expenses. Do not forget to add additional expenses like taxes, insurance, etc. that you pay only once or twice a year. Hopefully, you end up with money left over. Congratulations, you just created your budget. Now you can begin to determine how much money you can save.

Cutting back does not necessarily mean giving something up all together, but rather finding a less expensive way to do it. Let us say, for example, that each morning you stop by your favorite coffee shop and buy a cafe latté. It costs $3.00, or $15.00 per week. Another option is that you could stop by a local convenience store and buy your coffee for $1.00. You would save $10.00 per week or $520.00 per year. Not bad for a minor adjustment. If you took the $10.00 savings each week and invested it at a 5 percent return, after 20 years you would have over $17,600.00. Not bad for altering one buying habit. Most people have more than one cup of coffee a day. Just think of those savings. You could even make your own coffee at work, which would save you even more.

Below you will find ideas on where to start. If you think long and hard, I know you will be able to come up with many of your own ideas. I can assure you that if you are not already doing the things below, you will easily be able to save thousands of dollars a year. There are also some tips on saving time and aggravation.

Automobile

➢ Many car service centers recommend that you should have your oil changed every 3,000 miles. Check your owner's manual, based on your driving pattern. Many cars do not require an oil change until 7,500 miles, yet many dealers still tell you 3,000 miles. If you drive 15,000 miles per year, and each oil change costs $25.00, you could save $75.00 because you would require three less oil changes per year. If you invested the $75.00 savings at a 5 percent return for 20 years, you would accumulate over $2,500.00.

➢ Save money by keeping your vehicle properly tuned up, keeping tires properly inflated, and maintaining regular wheel alignment. Any one of these issues will cause you to lose a few miles per gallon of gas. How many miles per gallon depend on the seriousness of the problem. Misfiring spark plugs can reduce your fuel efficiency by over 30%.

➢ Do not spend money for higher octane-grade gasoline. It usually does not make much of a difference. Most cars do not get much better mileage, etc. that would justify the added cost. (Be sure to check your owner's manual and with the dealer's service department, when purchasing a new car. Not following their recommendations could void your warranty.)

➢ Be cautious before changing the wheel size of your vehicle to accommodate wider or larger sized tires. The larger tire size may only be available from a few manufacturers, which generally results in higher prices due to the lack of competition. This will be a recurring expense every time you need new tires. You may also have a hard time finding a replacement in a pinch.

➢ Most car alarms are not worth the cost. I conducted a test where I set off my alarm multiple times in a crowded parking lot and not one person stopped to question me or called the police. The lights were flashing and the alarm was very loud. If you feel you really need an alarm, make sure you get one that disables the starter or engine. They do save you money on insurance premiums, but will not pay for themselves with the discount received. The savings on your insurance premium is usually about ten to twenty-five dollars.

➤ If you are really concerned about your vehicle, consider a LoJack. This is a great tool for recovering your car. The way it works is that after you report your vehicle stolen they transmit a code to the receiver installed in your vehicle. At that point the LoJack in your vehicle transmits a signal that can be picked up by the police. Cars are usually recovered in less than five hours. It costs more than most alarms but the success rate is much better for getting your vehicle returned. The only problem is that once in a while the vehicle may have already been taken to a chop shop. (Check with LoJack customer services to find out if coverage is provided in your area.)

➤ Some gas stations offer credit cards that provide three to four percent cash back on the total price of your gas purchase. If you spend $15.00 per week on gas, and you invested the 3 percent rebate at 5 percent, for 20 years, you would accumulate over $790.00.

➤ I think everyone should have a cell phone in his or her car in case of an emergency. I am not saying to run out, buy a new cell phone, and pay a monthly fee. You can look for old cell phones that are no longer in use. Even though these phones cannot be used for other calls, you should still be able to connect to "911" services. I recommend getting a power adapter for the cell phone that plugs into the cigarette lighter, so you do not have to worry about batteries.

- From time to time, we all hit those nasty potholes in the road. When you go to the repair shop, they usually will tell you that you have a bad rim and it must be replaced. I have learned that, in many cases, the rim can be straightened out to the point that it is still usable. The repair shops do not seem to like to do this. Talk to the mechanic who is working on the vehicle. Slip them a few bucks if they get it fixed. (This will not work on aluminum wheels.)

- Always keep two pieces of cloth in your vehicle, one white and the other red. The cloths should be about 18 inches long by 5 inches wide. They can be used in the event your vehicle breaks down and you need assistance. Place the white cloth on the door handle, window, or antenna. Use the red cloth if there is snow present. The cloth will let police and others know that you need help. This is most effective on roads that are heavily traveled.

- Look for free or cheaper priced parking. If you go a few blocks out of your way, you can usually save half the cost of parking. You may even be able to park for free. Remember, exercise is good for your health

- Removing items from your car, that are not needed, will reduce the overall weight and gas consumption. For every one hundred pounds, you reduce your mileage per gallon by 1 to 2 percent.

- Accelerating gradually, when driving, will decrease gas usage. This can increase your mileage by two to five miles per each gallon of gas. Utilizing cruise control or overdrive on long trips will save you 5% to 10% per gallon. Driving at high speeds in low gear can increase gas consumption by 40%.

- Some cities are starting to use roadside cameras to take a picture of your license plate when you are speeding or go through a red light. You can add an anti-photo radar license plate cover to prevent your picture being taken. The license plate can easily be seen from the rear, but it appears blurry when looked at from the side or overhead. They only take a few minutes to install. The camera only takes a picture of the car's license plate and rear lights. It does not know who is in the car. In some states these are illegal so check your local laws. I have heard that if you are willing to sign an affidavit indicating you were not driving the vehicle at the time, they will drop the case. You will need to check into this further. If interested conduct a search on the Web for "anti-photo radar license plates."

➤ If you have to pay to park at a meter in front of your business, you may consider applying for a parking permit. If your business requires you to drive around in congested areas where parking is at a premium, you may want to check into a parking permit. This could save you a great deal of time, aggravation, and from possible fines you could receive at expired parking meters. Let us assume that your permit costs $600.00 per year, and normal parking fees are $12.00 per day. If you invested the $48.00, which is your weekly savings, at 5 percent for 20 years, you would end up with over $94,500.00 in the bank. This does not take into account tickets you might otherwise incur or fees for parking in more than one location each day.

➤ New tires have 10/32 of an inch of tread. By law, tires must be replaced when they have 2/32 of an inch of tire tread remaining. Most tires, however, tend to lose their traction when driving in rain or snow when they reach 4/32 of an inch. There are wear bars to indicate when the tire is worn. If the wear bars are equal to the tire tread the tire should be replaced. You can also use a penny to check the tread wear. Place Lincoln's head into the grooves; if the top of his head is visible, the tire should be replaced. You can also use a tire tread gauge for greater accuracy.

Check a few areas around the tire for best results.
(Vehicles start to hydroplane around 35 mph.)

➢ Over the years I have found that when you take your
vehicle in for an estimate or repair, the shop always seems
to find additional items that are in need of repair or
replacement. Most of the time they are things that you
were not even aware of because there was no discernable
effect on your cars' performance. If you use the following
phrases, mechanics will often change their mind, unless,
of course, the item is really bad.

> "I'm surprised, I just had it checked a few weeks
> ago and was told that it was OK. Are you sure?"

> "I'm not having any problems that I'm aware off.
> Could you show me the part that has the problem?
> What exactly will this affect if I do not get it fixed
> now? Are you sure this needs to be repaired
> now?"

Many mechanics tend to make suggestions about
replacing parts based on the mileage on your car, and
when other similar vehicles required the same repairs. It is
good to be proactive, but not if it is going to cost you a lot
of money for something that may not cause you to break
down.

You should regularly have parts inspected. Mechanics do
not consider your driving habits or how often the vehicle
is used. For example, if you drive your car for ten to
fifteen minutes each way to work you will probably need
to replace the parts in the exhaust system much sooner
than drivers that travel over forty-five minutes each way.
The reason is that condensation builds up in the exhaust
pipes and muffler, which leads to corrosion. When you
run a vehicle for a long period, the moisture buildup dries
from the high heat. So make sure to take a longer drive at
least once a month.

> Many times when you arrive at tollbooths, you tend to follow the rest of the cars and wait in long lines. As you approach the pay booth look towards the far right. There are often lanes not being used, or there are fewer vehicles using them. Also consider getting in line behind large tractor-trailers. Those lines tend to move faster. Keep in mind that when one tractor-trailer moves on, it is like four cars moving on.

> Look for or start a carpool for going to work daily. This will not only save you on gas, but also wear and tear on your vehicle.

> Not using the air conditioning and opening windows saves gas. This will increase your mileage by 1 to 3 miles per gallon. It can reduce gas consumption by as much as 18% depending on your vehicle.

> Before taking your vehicle in for inspection look it over yourself. You could easily turn on all the lights to ensure that all the bulbs are working. Bulbs are usually easy to replace. Check you wipers and make sure the window is clean and free of smears after use. Grease and dirt collect on windshields during dry weather and streaks when it rains. Use a non-abrasive cleaner to remove the residue build up on the window and the rubber wiper blade. If that does not do the trick, replace the wiper blades. (Wiper blades should be replaced at least once a year) The sun causes the rubber blade to deteriorate and become harder over time. Check these things all year round to ensure your safety and the safety of others.

> For those of you who believe in speeding, driving slower will lower your gas consumption. Once you exceed 60 miles per hour, your gas consumption is much higher. You could save 20% or more by driving 55 mph rather than 70 mph. (It takes four times as much horsepower to double your mph. For example if are driving at 20 mph using 15 horsepower, it would take you 60 horsepower to go 40

mph.) If you still insist on speeding, you might benefit from a good radar detector. Valentine One makes a radar detector that actually tells you the direction the radar signals are coming from (front, rear, or sides). It is a bit pricey but it is well worth the cost. Radar detectors are illegal in some states, check with local laws. These Web sites may also helpful.

www.SpeedTrap.org   www.BearTraps.com

➢ Whenever you rent a car you are asked if you want to buy the additional insurance coverage for accident or damage to the rental. These fees tend to be from $4.50 to $9.50 per day. If you already have car insurance, your existing policy will most likely cover you. Check with your insurance carrier. When charging the cost of the rental car, your credit card company may provide insurance coverage. If you do not have insurance, take the full coverage.

➢ I have realized that not all gasoline brands are the same even though they may have the same octane level. Some do not seem to provide as good mileage per gallon. Buying the cheapest may not be the cheapest in the end if it means you consume more gas. I get about 50 more miles to a tank of gas, when I use a certain brand of gas in my car. What you need to do is experiment with different types of gas and see if one is better than another, in your car. In order to do this, use up most of the gas in the tank, then fill up with a new brand. Do this at least two times. The third time, write down your odometer reading or reset the trip odometer, if you have one. You are now in the process of running your test. You should drive smoothly, do not be hard on the gas pedal. Drive the car until you are almost out of gas. When you fill up, write down your present mileage from the odometer you originally used. Subtract the new miles from the old and hold on to that number. Now write down the exact number of gallons, including tenths, that it took to fill your tank. Now, divide the number of miles by the number of gallons. The answer is the amount of mpg (miles per gallon). The higher the mpg, the better the gas in your car. I like to conduct this test twice. It is very important not to confuse your different driving habits and changes in road conditions that influence the mpg. Perform this test with other brands. The average person drives 12,000 miles per year. If you use cheap gas, that gets fewer mpg, you would require an additional four or more tanks of gas to reach that 12,000-mile mark. This Web site may help you find some low priced gasoline stations in your area.

www.FuelEconomy.gov

➤ Think about keeping your present car an extra year or two.

Dining

➤ Look for restaurant coupons, like two-for-one deals, in local magazines. If you eat out a great deal, buy a local coupon book. They usually pay for themselves after two or three meals.

➤ Let the host or hostess know if there is a certain area in the restaurant where you would like to be seated. If you are making reservations, let them know your seating preference in advance. Many times he/she may say they do not have any tables in that location available. Tell them you would really like to sit in one of those areas and you are willing to wait a little.

➤ Many restaurants have "early bird specials" from 4PM - 6PM. Some of the meals cost less during these times. In some cases, the portions are smaller.

➤ Charge your meals on credit cards that pay you cash back. This way you could save even more. Let us say you spend $200.00 a month on a credit card that gives you 3 percent back. If you take the 3 percent savings, and invest it at 5 percent, for 20 years, you will end up saving over $2,430.00. That will pay for a few good meals. Even when not investing the savings, you would save $72.00 dollars a year.

➢ Sometimes you use a coupon which states "Purchase One Entrée at Regular Price, and Get the 2nd Entrée* at Half Price" (*Of Equal or Lesser Value). When only two people are dining, there is no problem. When there are three or more people, many restaurants try to give you half off the lowest priced entrée. Insist that they apply the coupon to your two most expensive entrees.

➢ You can find delicious inexpensive meals in some of the ethnic neighborhoods (Chinatown, Little Italy, etc.). Ask people in the area to recommend good and reasonable restaurants where the locals go to eat. Stay away from the tourist traps. Did you ever notice that many of the restaurants in areas with a lot of tourism traffic are not very good? That is because they do not have to count on regular customers coming back so they can get away with it.

➢ If you want to go to an expensive restaurant, try going at lunchtime. You can often get the same food at a more affordable price.

➢ Drink water with meals.

➢ If you are planning an event, a new restaurant will usually offer you a much better price. They will usually be willing to bend over backwards to accommodate your needs.

➢ Check out the Travel section later in this chapter for extensive information on tipping.

➤ How many times have you gone out to dinner or to an affair and wondered which silverware you should use for each course? This should help clear up some of your questions. Forks will always be placed to the left side of the plate and knives will be on the right side. If the place setting in front of you has two forks and two knives (blades facing in), use the outermost fork and knife to eat the appetizer or salad (the salad fork has a thicker tine at the left to be used for cutting salads or greens). Then use the innermost fork and knife for the main course.

Two exceptions are soupspoons and oyster, or shellfish, forks. The soupspoon will be on the right, to the outside of the knives, and an oyster, or shellfish, fork will be to the right of the soupspoon, with the angle facing in (or to the right of the knives, if no soupspoon is needed). Traditionally, an oyster or shellfish appetizer is served first, then soup, followed by salad, and then the main course, so all the silverware is arranged in this order.

If you are served cheese, an additional knife and fork are required. They are usually added after the main meal is cleared away. If they are in place at the start of the meal, the cheese fork and cheese knife will be the fork and knife located closest to the plate.

A dessert fork and/or dessert spoon is placed above the top of your plate, parallel to the table edge (the fork should be pointing to the right and the spoon in the opposite direction). Sometimes dessert utensils are only brought to the table with the dessert itself.

Your bread and butter plate belongs on the left side at the 10:00 position. The butter knife should be sitting across the top of the butter plate. The water goblet is located at the 1:00 position on the right side. You may have two other goblets, one for red wine, and the other for white wine. The red wine goblet is below the water goblet and to the left side (in the middle). The white wine goblet is below the red and to the left.

I know you are wondering by now what all this has to do with saving money, time, and aggravation. Just picture going out to dinner for a job interview with an important client, or trying to impress your fiancé's parents for the first time. Sometimes etiquette plays an important part in our daily lives. People make decisions about us based on strange things. The job you are applying for may involve entertaining clients. It could cost you that job just because the first impression you gave was not good. You may even hear about it 10 years after you are married, during an unrelated discussion. 'He/she was trying to impress us that night yet he/she kept using all the wrong silverware and plates.' You never know when it could come back to haunt you.

Education

> If your children plan to go to college, start looking into colleges when they are at the end of their sophomore year. Visit a college or two to get a feeling for what the college is like. Ask the schools to explain their requirements and policies for admission. If possible, speak to a department head or admissions counselor to discuss your child's scholastic plans. Let them know what elective courses he/she has taken and their planned course for the next two years. Ask the counselor if they feel your child should modify his/her courses in any way. Ask if they have any recommendations that could help increase your child's chances of acceptance. Keep in touch by E-mail. It is best to do this early so your child has plenty of time to make adjustments in his/her curriculum.

> You can attend some colleges for free. You need to live in that state and meet the residency requirements. It could be

worth the relocation cost or delaying college until the requirements are met.

> ➤ I strongly believe that you need to start saving for your child's college expenses the day he/she is born. College costs just keep skyrocketing. They rise much faster than the rate of inflation. There are many plans to help you save money for education. Some even offer you tax breaks. Some of the investment plans available include the Uniform Gifts to Minors Act (UGMA); Educational Individual Retirement Account (EIRA), also now known as Coverdell Education Savings Accounts (ESA); 529 plans; and Upromise. Upromise is a new way of saving for college. If you register with the Web site, you can earn rebates on your everyday spending from thousands of companies. Upromise collects the rebates and helps you deposit them into a 529 account that you can use for your children's education. See Upromise for details.

www.upromise.com

> ➤ If you are planning to go to college, consider volunteering at businesses, hospitals, etc. which provide *scholarship* money.

> ➤ Many locations such as movie theaters, museums, travel agencies, mass transit systems, etc. give discounts if you are a student and have ID to prove it. This applies to adult students as well.

> ➤ There is another way you can save even if you already take full advantage of the education savings plans. Let us say you have an investment that you bought five years ago. If you sell that investment today you would have to pay taxes on the profits, or gain, at your tax rate. If, on the other hand, you gift the investment to your child to use for education, your child would be liable for the tax at his/her tax rate (which is usually lower than yours). There is an annual limit on the amount you can give as a gift without

having to pay a Federal Gift tax. Check your local tax regulations.

➤ Many people are under the impression that their children will never be able to attend some of the prestigious colleges because of the cost. Many of these colleges and universities are "need blind" and will work out financial aid if your child is accepted for admission. Grants, loans, and scholarships may also be available.

➤ If you have a fair amount of money in the bank or in stocks, consider saving additional money towards your retirement, if you are not already putting aside the maximum. This will help lower the amount of your overall assets when applying for financial aid. Retirement accounts are not considered when they are determining the amount of your assets. The money must be in a qualified retirement account. If you open a Roth IRA, you can still withdraw the original money you invested after five years without penalty. However, you will not be able to take any interest that has accumulated. Parents are required to contribute about 5 percent of their assets for college each year. Children must contribute about 35 percent of their assets for each year of college. This payment is known as the *Expected Family Contribution* (EFC). Use this Web site to calculate your EFC.

www.finaid.org/calculators/

➤ If your child has earned a Bachelor's degree, is over twenty-one, and is seeking further education, *Federal aid* is computed using his/her salary and assets rather than those of the parents and child combined. This means that more Federal aid will probably be available, and out of pocket expenses will probably be less.

➤ Below are Web sites that can help you with college related information. The Web sites are usually in lower case letters, but I like to capitalize the first letter in the name or word because it makes it easier to remember that way. These sites include a wide range of information on colleges, scholarships, financial aid, loans and loan consolidation, job needs in your market, saving for college, college credits for work experience, and many other interesting facts. If you look through these sites, you will also find links to many other good sites.

www.CollegeSavings.org
www.WiredScholar.com
www.Istudentloan.com
www.cael.org
www.NellieMae.com
www.SavingForCollege.com
www.StudentClearinghouse.org
www.StudentLoanFunding.com
www.LoanConsolidation.ed.gov

www.fafsa.ed.gov
www.FastWeb.com
www.FinAid.com
www.AceNet.edu
www.dol.gov
www.SallieMae.com

Financial

> Keep your costs down by buying stock indexes. (I own some of these myself.) They usually have a much lower expense ratio. I also think they are better for the average investor because you are not purchasing a single company's stock. They offer more diversity than buying one or two single stocks. An index represents a portfolio of stocks, grouped in a particular way (the S&P 500 Index (SPY) is made up of large-capitalization stocks; the Russell 2000 Index (IWM) includes small-capitalization stocks; Nasdaq-100 (QQQQ), and Dow Jones Industrial (DIA) are just a few others). There are many to choose from but be sure to do your research before investing. I like them better than actively managed funds because you often do not have to pay capital gains taxes every year. If you insist on buying actively managed funds, look for "no load" funds with no account maintenance fees.

- ➤ Do not get involved in the stock market unless you are prepared to lose the money you invest. Always diversify your investments and do not get greedy. Do not put money in the market unless you do not need it for at least five to ten years. See this site for some information on indexes. There are many other sites.

  www.IndexFunds.com

- ➤ Today there are many ways to buy stocks, options, funds, etc. Shop around for the best deals. You no longer need to pay stockbrokers ridiculous fees that make them rich at your expense. The Internet has some of the best sites, and you can find deals that require minimal opening balances to start. You can find deals for under $6.00 per transaction to buy or sell stock.

  In some cases you can buy stock directly from the company, rather than through a broker, and you can eliminate all fees. These stocks are sometimes referred to as DPPs (*Direct Purchase Plan*). Some companies even offer *Dividend Reinvestment Plans* (DRIPs). DRIPs allow you to buy your stock straight from the company, as long as you already own at least one share of that company's stock. Some companies even give you the opportunity to buy their stock at a 2 to 5 percent discount off the market price. This usually applies when shares are purchased with reinvested dividends. The amount of stock that you can buy is limited. The difference between a DRIP and a DPP is that to buy a DRIP, you must already own at least one share of the company's stock so you can reinvest your dividends for more shares of that stock. A first-time buyer can buy a DPP. The Web sites below have information on DRIPs and DPPs.

  www.netstockdirect.com   www.enrolldirect.com
  www.dripinvestor.com   www.dripadvisor.com
  www.wall-street.com/directlist.html

> Financial advisors are not always the best source of advice. They use your money to invest and if they lose your money they, themselves do not lose much. If financial advisors really had confidence in making you money then they would only charge commissions on the money they earn for you. Instead, they usually want a percentage of the total amount of money you have invested with them, whether they make money for you or lose your money. Some only make money on your transactions. The more transactions, the more money they make. I would rather pay them a fee of five percent on the money they make for me. Unfortunately no one out there, that I am aware of, is willing to do that in today's world.

> One of the most important things in keeping your financial health in order is to ensure that your credit history is up to date and in good standing. If you have not looked at your credit report in the last three years, I would recommend you do so. Many companies turn to your credit history before giving you a new job, credit card, loan, insurance, etc. Too many of these reports do not reflect accurate data about you and your credit history, yet companies use them regularly. That is why it is important to look at the report yourself and have all discrepancies resolved and removed. Discrepancies may occur for many reasons, such as outdated records, misinformation from others, confusion with others of similar names or accounts, typing mistakes, etc.

Most companies use just three of the many credit bureau companies out there. I would recommend getting reports from all three of the most used in your area. Below are sites where you can get a copy of your credit report for a small fee and in some cases for free. I also think it is a good idea to know your FICO score, especially if you are planning to apply for a loan. If you have a good score, you will probably qualify for better interest rates. Some of the Web sites offer you the opportunity to contact the three bureaus at once, for one fee. Check out these sites and see which best suit your needs.

www.Equifax.com   www.TransUnion.com
www.Experian.com   www.Qspace.com
www.TrueCredit.com   www.MoniTrust.com

➤   Many companies like to run credit reports to see if you qualify for a loan, vehicle purchase, credit card, etc. Do not let these people make credit inquiries unless you are definitely interested in doing business with that company. Too many inquiries can prevent you from being approved for something. Businesses can be fined, by the FTC, if they proceed with credit inquiries without your approval. Keep in mind that when you apply for a mortgage at an Internet site that promises two to six lender responses, each potential lender will most likely run a separate credit report.

➤   If you need to keep a minimum balance in your bank, consider keeping it in a Money Market account. They usually pay much higher interest rates. They are not all insured by Federal Deposit Insured Corporation (FDIC) but the money should be very safe in these types of accounts. Some banks, brokerage accounts, and credit unions allow you to tie your checking or debit card to a Money Market account. This is a good way to make money on your money, even if it costs you a few dollars a month. Most are free.

➤   If you have a high interest rate on your mortgage or loan, consider refinancing. Shop around for lower rates. In some cases you can refinance your mortgage for a lower interest rate and without paying any points or closing costs. The difference between a 7% and 11%, 15 year, $100,000.00 loan is $242.77 in your monthly payment. If you invested that money each month at 5% interest, over the life of your loan, you would have over $64,000.00. Better yet, apply it towards your monthly mortgage principle and receive a better return.

> Every once in a while, credit card companies offer interest free cash advances for a small fee. If you have a high credit limit, it is probably worth taking their money and investing it for a short period of time. If you time it right, you can hold onto their money for about fifty days.

Let us say you have a credit limit of $25,000.00, and the credit card company charges you a one-time fee of $10.00 for a cash advance. If you borrow the $25,000.00 and invest it for 45 days, you could end up with a net profit of over $140.00. Not bad for using their money. (Make sure to invest it in something with guaranteed interest, where the principal is not in danger of being lost.) Be sure to pay the cash advance back on time so that you do not owe interest fees.

> If you are married, you should have all commonly owned items in both of your names (deeds, legal documents, titles, insurance policies, etc.). This will help protect your assets if you are sued. It is especially important if you work in a field that is considered at risk (police officer, doctor, nurse, security guard, etc.). Your employer does not always cover you.

> A will is important if you have assets that you would like to pass on to others when you pass away. Not having a will creates a great deal of aggravation for your loved ones, not to mention that the hard earned money and assets that you own will be heavily taxed. A will may not be what you need, however, depending on the amount of assets you control. To get the best advice on this topic you should seek a lawyer who specializes in estate planning. Many lawyers provide a free half-hour to 1-hour consultation to determine if they are qualified for the job. Ask them about their fees before getting started. Ensure that he/she has been practicing estate planning for at least

five years, and that they have handled many cases involving the type of will or trust that you choose. If your net worth is over two million dollars, look for a lawyer that has at least ten years of experience. These sites may help you with legal information and lawyer referrals.

www.abanet.org   www.LawSource.com

➢ If your spouse should pass away and leave you holding accounts that contain stocks, funds, bonds, etc., have a good financial planner look over all of the assets. Ask them to ensure that your money is being invested in something that is not at risk. Do not assume that because your spouse had those assets they will always be safe. Things can change very quickly.

➢ Are you giving the IRS (Internal Revenue Service) free money out of your paycheck? Many of us have the wrong amount of taxes withheld from our checks. If you receive a large tax refund check at the end of the year, then you are probably one of those folks. If you kept that money, you could invest it throughout the year. Request a W-4 form from your employer and change your withholding rate. (Be careful not to take back more than you are entitled to. If you do you may have to pay a penalty on the additional amount.) If you get back $2,000.00 a year from the IRS, it means that you are giving them a $38.46 free loan from your weekly paycheck. If you kept that money and invested it at 5 percent, over 20 years, you would earn more than $1,600.00 in interest.

➢ If your company retirement program includes a company match to your contributions, be aware of some potentially confusing issues. The Internal Revenue Service (IRS) sets a limit on your annual pretax contribution to the plan. That figure can change each year. If your company matches a portion of your contribution, the amount they contribute does not count towards your IRS limit for that year. Be sure to arrange your contributions to continue over a twelve-month period. Below are two examples. The first shows the way you should do it, and the second shows how you can lose money by not spreading out your contributions. Both examples are based on the following information: you earn $100,000.00 per year, there are 26 pay periods, the IRS limit for contributions for the year is $12,000.00, and your company matches 6 percent. The company permits you to contribute up to 20% of your biweekly gross pay of $3,846.15. These numbers are for illustration only and are not meant to reflect actual IRS guidelines.

Example 1
I am contributing 12% of my gross pay and the company matches 6%. Each pay period I contribute $461.53.
After 26 pay periods I reach my contribution limit of $12,000.00.
The company matches $230.76 each pay period or $6,000.00 for the year.

Example 2
I am contributing 20% of my gross pay and the company matches 6%. Each pay period I contribute $769.23.
After 15 pay periods I have put in $11,538.45 and in the 16th pay period I am only allowed to contribute $461.55, which puts me at the $12,000.00 limit.
The company matches $230.76 per pay period that I contribute. After 16 pay periods, once I have reached the maximum contribution, the company stops contributing. The company contributed a total of $3,692.16 for the year.

In both examples, I contributed $12,000.00. But in example 1, the company match was $2,307.34 more than in example 2. So be sure to examine the details of your company plan carefully before making your investment decisions.

➢ When you get married, you are entitled to some extra tax refunds for the entire year, when you file jointly, even if the wedding takes place in December.

➢ There are places that list names of people who have money owed to them for one reason or another. See if you or a family member is on the list. This is just one of the sites you can check.

www.MissingMoney.com

➢ You can claim a newborn child on your taxes for the entire year, even if that child is born on December 31.

➢ Open a flexible reimbursement account for Health Care and Dependent Care if your employer offers these plans. You can set aside money from your paycheck that will be used to pay for products and services. The money that you use is considered pre-tax dollars (you do not pay federal taxes on this money). This will lower the amount of taxes you need to pay at the end of the year. It may even put you in a lower tax bracket. If you can take advantage of these kinds of accounts, you could save thousands. The higher your tax bracket, the more you will save.

➢ When you finish paying off a loan, continue to make the payments, but now to yourself. Place the money into a new or existing savings account. Watch it continue to grow as you add money regularly and it accumulates interest. Let us say you just paid off a $15,000.00 loan for which you were paying $190.01 monthly. If you continue to put that money aside each month, and invest it at 5 percent, after 10 years you will have over $29,000.00.

➢ Make sure that the designated beneficiary is up to date on all bank accounts, life insurance policies, *401K* plans or a will. You should check these items every time you have any major change in your lifestyle such as a new home, new job, birth of a child or grandchild, divorce or separation, change in health status, etc.

➢ Many people do not have a bank account and regularly pay 1.25% to 5% fees for check cashing. Find a bank that offers free checking and stop throwing away your money. Let us say you are paid $1,000.00 biweekly and you pay a 2% charge for cashing your paycheck. If you had a checking account, you could cash your check for free and save the 2%. If you invest the 2% you saved at 5 percent, over 20 years you will have more than $35,000.00.

➢ It is never too early to start saving for your retirement. The sooner the better. You could live thirty or more years after you retire. The only catch is that you need to earn money before you can invest money into a qualified retirement account.

➢ You should create a financial plan that includes your investments, retirement plans, social security, and savings accounts. Keep this together with the budget you created. This way you will always know your present financial situation. Be certain that it is kept up to date.

➢ Whenever you are signing contracts make sure you read them in detail and that you understand what each of the clauses mean. I know it takes a while to read these things, and they can be confusing. Ask questions. After all, they were written by lawyers and are probably purposely designed to confuse us. If the person presenting you the contract cannot explain it, tell them to get someone who can.

➢ If you are buying a new home you can save money by putting twenty percent down. This will prevent you from having to pay *Private Mortgage Insurance* (PMI), which is not tax deductible. The cost for PMI ranges from $45.00 to $150.00 per month. It depends on the amount of your loan and your down payment. The money would have a greater return for you if it were being applied towards the actual mortgage. If you did not have to pay $75.00 monthly PMI fees for 5 years, you could invest that money at 5% and you would have over $5,000.00. Better yet, apply it to your mortgage principle each month and save even more.

➢ For my next money saving idea you will need a large container. You can use an old pickle jar, coffee can, juice bottle, or one of those large water bottles. Empty the change from your pocket, or purse, on a daily basis and put it in the container. At first you may miss it, but after a week you will not notice the difference. You will be amazed by how much money you can save over the course of a year. This can easily add up to hundreds of dollars a year.

➢ Making one extra mortgage payment a year will save you thousands of dollars. If your mortgage rate is 7.5 percent and you add $50.00 extra to each monthly payment, it is like putting your money into a bank and earning 7.5 percent interest, tax-free (you will lose the tax deduction on that portion of interest, but you gain peace of mind by paying your house off sooner). If you have a 30-year (360 months) mortgage for $100,000.00, you will pay over $151,700.00 in interest over the life of the loan. If you add the additional $50.00 towards your principal each month, you will pay off your mortgage 71 months early and save over $35,600.00 in interest. The higher your interest rate, the more you save.

➢ If your work place has a retirement plan, take advantage of it by having regular amounts deducted from your paycheck each week. Over time you will not miss that money and you will eventually accumulate a great deal of money. In many states it will even reduce your taxable income, which will lower your taxes. (Check your local tax laws). Some companies actually match a percentage of what you contribute to their plan. That is usually somewhere between one and six percent. It is very important that you contribute whatever they are willing to match. It is like getting free money. If your annual salary is $60,000.00 and you contribute 18 percent and are in the 28 percent tax bracket, you can reduce your annual income tax by over $3,000.00. (Do not put all of your money in one stock when investing in retirement plans. If that stock fails, you could lose it all.)

➤ Open a Transportation Benefits Reimbursement Account if your work offers this type of plan. You can set aside money from your paycheck that will be used to pay for qualified expenses incurred when traveling to work. Parking, public transportation, and vanpool expenses qualify for reimbursement. It allows you to deduct parking expenses up to $200.00 per month and mass transit expenses up to $105.00 per month. The money deducted from your pay is pre-tax dollars. This lowers taxes you need to pay at the end of the year. It may even put you in a lower tax bracket. If you take full advantage of this program, you can save hundreds of dollars. You may even save over $1,000.00, depending on your tax bracket.

➤ Get the most out of the money you save by applying it towards your credit card balances, mortgages, and loans. It will go much further this way. You say you do not have any of these, that is great! Then open up an individual retirement account (IRA).

➤ All mortgage companies like to hold *escrow accounts* of your money that they use to pay your property taxes and homeowner insurance premiums. I would like to be in the business of holding people's money for free. Ask your mortgage holder if you can pay your taxes and insurance directly. If they say no, escalate the matter to upper management. Not all insurance companies allow you to do this. If they do, deposit the money into a money market account each month and you can earn interest on your money. If you held $4,000.00 a year in a bank account until you needed it to pay the tax and insurance bills, and that account earned 5 percent interest, you would accumulate over $5,000.00 in interest over the 30-year life of your mortgage.

➤ Below is a list of Web sites that can help you research stocks and funds. These sites include stock and fund information, ratings, financial terms, constant monitoring of your portfolio, and many other interesting facts. Look through these sites and you will find many useful links to other sites. There are many other sites out there, you just need to look.

www.Moodys.com	www.Morningstar.com
www.Fundsinteractive.com	www.Money.com
www.Bloomberg.com	www.FundAlarm.com
www.StandardandPoors.com	www.Quicken.com

Health

➤ If you belong to a health maintenance organization (HMO) that covers drugs and allows you to order a ninety-day supply for one fee-take advantage of it. Ask your doctor to write the prescription for a ninety-day supply.

➤ About half the states in the U.S. have some type of program to provide pharmaceutical coverage or assistance for low-income elderly persons or people with a disability.

➤ If you need to go to a hospital for any elective (non-emergency) procedure, be selective about which hospital you choose. The best advice may come from friends who work in the hospital. Some hospitals have much higher failure rates than others for certain procedures. The failures can be contributed to staffing issues, lack of training, funding, priorities, administrative issues, etc. Most of these issues, unfortunately, are not well known or publicized. You should ask for your doctor's opinion, especially if he/she practices at more than one hospital. Talk to others in the medical field. Call the hospital administrator and ask about the complication rates for the procedure you are going to have. Find out how that percentage compares to the average for other hospitals in your area. All hospitals should keep such statistics. If they do not, you probably do not want to deal with them. These Web sites below have some limited information on hospitals.

www.usnews.com   www.jcaho.org

> If you are a senior citizen below a certain income level, you may qualify for discounted drugs directly from the manufacturer. Find out who makes the drug you are using and contact the manufacturer's customer service department. Ask if they have a program that can help you. Your savings can add up to thousands of dollars. A well-known cholesterol-lowering drug can cost $320.00 for a 3-month supply. One of these programs offers the same drug and quantity for just $50.00. They also assist people who could not otherwise afford these medications. You can always ask for help from companies. You have nothing to lose, only to gain.

The Web site below is a good resource to help you in locating information on some of the drug companies that offer assistance.

www.NeedyMeds.com

> Check out some of the discount department stores that have pharmacies. They may offer prices lower than you are currently paying.

> You can order drugs at major discounts from the Internet, by mail, or by phone. Most of the companies are in Canada and Mexico. (United States law may consider this illegal.)

➤ Consider a generic drug, if available. Buying generic medications can save you from 40 to 70 percent off the brand name prices. Check with your doctor to determine which generic medications will work for you.

➤ Ask your doctor if he/she has any free samples of the medication that they prescribed for you.

➤ If you have been on a drug for many years, ask your doctor if you still need to take the drug, or if there are now less expensive drugs that can be prescribed.

➤ Many doctors and hospitals send bills for services performed that are not always clearly understood. You should keep track of all dates, doctors, labs, x-rays, treatments, hospitalizations, and services performed for your own records. When the bills come in try to match them up with your own records. Remember that one treatment or procedure can result in multiple bills, especially if you are in the hospital. Sometimes they may appear to be duplicates but actually are bills for different aspects of the same procedure. For example, if you have an operation as an out patient, it may involve the doctor or doctors who must perform the procedure, Medical Surgical supplies used for the operation and treatment after, lab testing, x-rays, operating room charges for the actual room, Anesthesiologist, pharmacy for medications used, and recovery room charges. It is possible to receive a separate invoice from each one of these areas. If you do not understand the bill, start by calling your doctors' billing department for an explanation.

You could save yourself some aggravation by asking why something is being done if the doctor did not make you aware of it. Keep in mind that any item you are given will most likely be billed for, so if you do not need it let them know. Sometimes mistakes are made and items are billed twice. Never pay your bill before the primary insurance company pays their share first. If you have a secondary insurance provider let them make their payment also. Many insurance providers negotiate lower fees for the procedure you were given. Make sure you understand your insurance company's benefits. Many companies continue to bill and send late notices until your insurance company pays their portion. Make sure you are not being charged twice. Do the dates match with the dates you were there? Are there charges for items or services not performed? Always investigate charges that are very high. Sometimes they punch in the wrong code, which could make a big difference in your charges. Sometimes you are charged for one box of pills when you only received one pill.

It helps to keep all of the bills filed in the following order: date of service, provider's name, service provided, charges, date submitted (by whom, the doctor, the hospital, etc.), amount paid (by primary insurer, and the date), date submitted (to secondary insurer, if applicable), amount paid (by secondary insurer and the date), and balance (what you must pay).

> Ask at pharmacies which organizations tend to get the most discounts, and consider joining those organizations. Ask at pharmacies if they offer senior citizen discounts.

> Some pills can be split in half. If you take 20mg. for example, you may be able to buy the 40mg. tablet for the same price and then cut them in half. Check with your doctor or pharmacist, not all tablets can be split. Splitting tablets can save you up to 100%. If a tablet does not have a scored line, it is not meant to be cut.

> Not all pharmacies have the same discounts on all drugs. Consider buying medications at more than one pharmacy.

> If you have a prescription drug plan and your doctor tells you to take an over-the-counter drug, you may ask your

doctor if they make a prescription that is similar, so that the cost will be covered under your plan.

➤ When your doctor writes a prescription for medication, ask the doctor to mark "Do not substitute." This does not allow the pharmacist to substitute a generic brand or formulary medication for the one your doctor ordered. This is important if you have been on medication that works well for you and you change insurance companies. They will often substitute a formulary medicine that may not work as well for you. If you are paying for the drug yourself and would prefer to purchase the generic, make sure they do not check "Do not substitute."

➤ Many products, such as over-the-counter drugs, can be purchased for a lot less than their name brand competitors. There are store brands that have the same active ingredients. Many of these products are made by the same manufacturer.

➤ Below is a list of Web sites that can help you with health-related issues. The Web sites are usually in lower case letters, but I like to capitalize the first letter in the name or word because it makes it easier to remember. These sites range from medical terms, descriptions of illness, disasters, new medical discoveries, and many other interesting facts.

www.HealthWeb.org	www.CDC.gov
www.FDA.gov/cder/drug	dirline.nlm.nih.gov
www.oncolink.upenn.edu	www.aoa.gov
www.nlm.nih.gov/medlineplus/	www.medicare.gov

Here are some other health sites related to dealing with disasters and how to cope with them.

www.nimh.nih.gov	www.aacap.org
www.fema.gov	www.apa.org
www.psych.org	www.usdoj.gov
www.ncptsd.org	

Home

➢ Do not pay others to do things you can easily do yourself such as cutting your grass, washing your car or shoveling the snow. Instead of paying someone $25.00 to cut your grass for 24 weeks each year, you could invest that money at 5 percent interest. Over 20 years you would accumulate over $20,000.00.

➢ Dust off light bulbs. Dust can cut down on light by forty percent. Use a dry cloth with the light bulb turned off. Applying moisture to a hot light bulb can cause it to explode.

➢ If you have a tree that is sick or deteriorating, you can call an arborist. Many arborists provide free estimates. They come to your home, let you know what is wrong, and quote a price to bring your tree back to health, if possible. The arborist you select should be state certified.

➢ Many of us would like the comfort of knowing that our homes are safe. You do not always have to pay a lot of money for a security system. In fact, if you go to a local alarm company, you can usually purchase window stickers or mailbox post signs for a minimal fee. Just place them in a very visible location at your home. This is often all you need to keep someone from breaking into your home.

➢ Are you renting an apartment or planning to share a house with others? Make sure that you have a signed agreement between all parties. It should spell out everything in detail. Who pays and how much do you pay for the rent? Are there late fees for late payments? Are utilities included? Are pets allowed? Are you allowed to have a visitor sleep over? Who pays the telephone bill? How much notice do you need to provide before moving? Who is responsible for repairs? This is just a sampling of the things that should be included. Many people say, "But we are friends." It does not matter. Things can change and sometimes we forget or disagree about what was agreed upon.

➢ Do you have appliances in your home that have condensation pipes that need to drain such as air conditioning and central air conditioning units? Check the drainage tubes regularly to ensure that they do not become clogged. If they clog, the backed-up water could drain elsewhere and ruin your carpet, furniture, and walls.

➢ Many of us waste products we use because we are lazy or in a rush. How many times have you thrown out that mustard or ketchup bottle, toothpaste tube, etc. before it was completely empty? Many times all you need to do is store the bottles upside down and you can easily get additional servings. Lay your toothpaste tube on a hard surface. Place your toothbrush handle at the bottom of the toothpaste tube. Now apply a little pressure while sliding it from the bottom of the tube towards the opening. Do this two or three times and you will probably get a few more days from your product. Please make sure the cap is on or you will have a mess on your hands.

➢ To avoid breakage of fragile glass, porcelain or ceramic figurines, try putting denture adhesive on the bottoms. This will help hold them on glass, mirror, or stone shelves. I recommend you first test this in an area that cannot be seen to make sure it does not damage the surface.

➢ Many neighborhoods have block parties. Local stores can donate most of the food, beverages, beer, and prizes. This is a nice way to have an annual party and allows stores in your area to show their appreciation for your business. Contact the stores early in the year and make them aware that you will be having a block party. Ask them to set aside some funds for your party. (The reason you want to contact them early is that if your party is in late summer they may have already spent their allocated budget by the time you talk to them.)

Call all of the stores and ask them for their fax number and the store manager's name. Create a general letter that will be sent to each business. See Figure A, below, for an example. Create a poster board with a list of all contributors and display it prominently at the party. This lets everyone know which businesses are giving back to the community.

Figure A

To whom it may concern (or the manager's name)

Our neighborhood will be having a block party on (Date). The people involved have shopped in your store. We live on (Street and Development name or area), which is located at (name two cross streets by your street, zip code xxxxx-xxxx). We would like to know if your establishment would be interested in contributing to our block party. We thank you for your consideration and will continue to use your store for our needs.

Some suggestions: gift certificates for your store, food, outdoor games, prizes for game winners, gifts for the children, beer, soda, and ice.

Thank You,

Your full name & address
xxxxxxxxxxxxx
xxxxxxxxxxxxx
Your phone number
E-mail address

It can be a small party or a big extravaganza. I know people who have had politicians and fire trucks show up. The children were able to check out the truck and equipment. They had pony rides, all kinds of games, and stands where you could win prizes. All the children received prizes, and even some of the adults. Do not overlook the banks. They often have coloring books or water bottles, etc. that they will donate. Some businesses contribute money but most allow you to choose items from their store, or may provide gift certificates. You may have to take up a small collection from the people coming to the party if you do not have enough donations.

Do not forget to thank all of the contributors after the party and let them know how much everybody enjoyed it. Also, tell them about the poster board you created and let them know that you advertised their name to all the attendees. This will help you in gaining donations the following year.

➤ When buying a new sofa, car or furniture with fabric, buy a fabric protector and spray the material, when new, according to the directions. Most future spills and stains will wipe right off.

➤ Hold a garage sale for all those unwanted items.

➤ Keep your sidewalks clear of snow and ice. Do not use ice-melting agents because they can damage concrete. Ice melting agents work by reducing the freezing process of water (the product used and temperature at the time are two very important factors). Unfortunately, ice-melting agents create more frequent freezing and thawing cycles, which causes spalling (surface scaling of concrete). When liquid changes to ice it expands approximately 9% and creates stress. When the ice melts (changes back to liquid), the stress is released. If you add salt the expansion rate doubles causing trapped water to damage the concrete. If you still choose to use an ice-melting agent, you could lessen the risk by removing slush as soon as it forms. You could also apply a concrete sealer a few months before winter starts. (Do not use melting agents on porous concrete or concrete less than one year old. Freshly poured concrete has a high water content even when it looks dry.) Most ice melting agents are not environmentally safe and can cause damage to grass, vegetation and even pollute wells, rivers, and streams. Some of the more common products contain sodium chloride (rock salt), calcium chloride, magnesium chloride, calcium magnesium, and potassium acetate. The agents that contain chloride can also cause metal to corrode. Make sure to wash your hands immediately after use. Read all directions and warnings on the package before use.

➢ Some people have told me they reuse their vacuum cleaner bags multiple times before replacing them. This can be done two ways depending on your bag style. Either way, do this outside over a trashcan. Remove the dirt through the opening where the bag attaches to the vacuum cleaner, if you can see it. On some bags this is not possible and you will need to pull the bag apart from the seam at the top or bottom. It is preferred that you do this at the top if you have a choice. Unravel the paper folds carefully, remove and discard the dirt. Re-fold the bag adding at least one additional fold and staple across the bag to hold it securely. Do not do this too many times because the vacuum cleaner will lose some of its suction power and the bag may burst open. If you are allergic to dirt and dust, I would not recommend doing this at all.

➢ If you own property check that you are not being over-charged for Real Estate Taxes. You can do this by finding other similar properties that have sold in your area in the past year. Compare the results by calling your local tax collector's office and ask them what the current *Market Value* of your property is for assessment purposes. If the Tax Collector's figure is much greater than the cost you came up with, then you should file a *Property Tax Appeal*. You want to let them know that your property tax assessment is too high based on other similar property selling at the *Fair Market Value* in your area. In some cases this can only be done at certain times of the year. You can get this information from real estate offices, newspapers, the Internet, etc. Be prepared to take your appeal to the next level if you are denied. The higher you go the better your chances and the better your discount.

➢ Many times you can donate items to a local charity and receive a tax deduction. This is a good thing because you are also helping others who are less fortunate. Think twice before throwing something out. Your trash could be somebody else's fortune. Helping others will make you feel good. This can save you hundreds of dollars on your tax return.

➢ Consider installing a water alarm indicator for your sump pump or water heater, which will sound if the water leaks, or the level is too high. These devices can be built for as little as $7.00, or buy one already assembled for about $25.00. This will alert you to a potentially serious problem before damage occurs.

➢ Some people have a choice and pay for their own trash hauling. Most trash haulers offer multiple packages to select from. Most of us tend to have our trash picked up twice a week. Do you really have that much trash or could you get away with once a week. You could save five or more dollars per month by selecting once a week. If you save $5.00 per month and invest it at 5%, in 20 years you would save over $2,000.00.

➢ Make sure that you buy smoke detectors and *carbon monoxide detectors* for your home, apartment, and business. Place them in all locations as per the directions. It could save you lots of money one day, not to mention saving your life or the life of one of your family members. The carbon monoxide detector actually saved my whole family one winter night. Periodic cleaning may be required if dust builds up. Carbon monoxide detector sensors usually have a 5 to 10 year lifespan. The sensors become more sensitive with age. In addition, change your batteries at least once a year.

➤ Black top driveway sealers are packaged as ready to use. However, sealers are sometimes overused. Applying a thick coating will cause damage even though it looks great. If you build it up to the point where it starts to support itself, it will crack. If the driveway is less than three years old it needs to breathe and may start to crack when it becomes hot enough. You should apply sealer every two or three years. Some experts say every five years, but it really depends on the climate in which you live. Do not seal a new driveway until nine months to a year after it is installed.

➤ If you have a fireplace, close the *flue damper* tightly when not in use. An open damper is like having a window wide open in your house. If you do not use the fireplace, you may want to seal the area so you do not lose heat in the winter. Do not forget to remove the seal later if you plan to use it again. Remove it when you sell the house. It can be deadly if someone starts a fire and the flue cannot be opened.

➤ If you have a roaring fire in your fireplace, you can lose as much as 20,000 cubic feet of air per hour. That air must be replaced with the cold air from outside. Your heating system will need to run more often to keep the house warm. Lower the thermostat if possible.

➤ Test Ground Fault Interrupter (GFI), or Ground Fault Circuit Interrupter (GFCI), protection outlets in your home at least once a quarter to ensure your safety. (GFI circuits protect you from getting shocked.) This is done by plugging an electrical appliance into the outlet and turning it on. Then press the test button (usually black, could be yellow or white) and the appliance should turn off within a second. If your appliance turns off, the outlet is safe to use. If not, have an electrician check it out. To reset (turn the power back on) you will need to press the reset button (usually red). The appliance should turn back on. If it does not, have an electrician check it out. When testing a GFI circuit breaker you will need to turn the breaker all the way off, after you pushed the test button, before you can turn it back on again. I would recommend you have GFI protection outlets for all outdoor outlets, and anywhere inside the house where you may be exposed to water (near kitchen sink, wet basement, bathrooms, garage, etc.). Some outlets are fed by a GFI breaker out of your electrical panel. Other GFI outlets could be in another part of the home, which may feed two or more other outlets on the same branch circuit.

➤ If you sell any item to another party make sure you create a receipt. It should include the person's name who you are selling the item to, how much they paid for it, if they are paying the item off over time - explain the details, if you are giving them a warranty - write down the details and when will it expire. If you are not giving the person a warranty, make sure the receipt says, "This item is being sold AS IS, with no warranty expressed or given." The seller and buyer should both sign the receipt.

➤ Use water savers on faucets. Place a plastic bottle filled with water in toilet water tank to cut down on water usage. Older toilets use 5-6 gallons per flush. This can be lowered by about a gallon, depending on the size of the plastic bottle you use. An average household of four uses 250 gallons of water per day. Forty percent is used by toilets and thirty-five percent is used by other bathroom needs (faucets, bath, shower). Water savers can cut water usage to 1.5 to 2.5 gallons per minute. Without water savers, water usage averages 5 gallons per minute.

➤ Close the heat/air vents in rooms that are unoccupied. Do not close too many vents in the house because it can harm your heating and air system. This can save you 5% to 8% on your bill.

➤ Consider adding a whole house fan. It draws a large volume of outside air into the house through open windows or doors. Use it instead of air conditioning when the outside air is cool enough. The breeze created by fans allows you to raise the temperature by 5 degrees and still feel comfortable. A typical whole house fan costs 3-5 cents per hour to operate, while air conditioning costs 22 to 25 cents per hour. These fans can reduce costs by 70 percent.

Also, add an attic fan, which will help to keep the space below the roof from becoming too hot. The fans usually run on an automatic thermostat and require no human intervention.

➢ Turn off all electronic equipment, appliances, and lights in the house that are not being used. Use *motion sensors* for outdoor lighting whenever possible.

➢ You can save money by buying the new *fluorescent bulbs*. The bulbs cost more but they are well worth the price. They last at least five times longer and consume less electricity in comparison to *incandescent bulbs*. They also operate much cooler. They should fit most lamps and fixtures. Check for the *lumens* (light output) you need and select the bulb with the lowest wattage rating. Also compare the lumens ratings between bulbs, because some may not be as bright for the same power consumption. The higher the number, the more light it gives off. If you use a 60-watt incandescent bulb for 4 hours a day, in one year you would consume 87.6 kWh of electric power. On the other hand, if you used an 18-watt fluorescent bulb (60-watt bulb incandescent equivalent) you would only use 26.28 kWh over that same time. You would use 61.32 kWh less power and the lumens would be even brighter. That is a savings of about $8.00 per year on one bulb. Check your local rate for your savings. Fluorescent bulbs will lose some of their lumens as they get older.

➢ Install dimmer switches for incandescent lights in rooms that do not always need the maximum brightness.

➤ Turn your thermostat down in the winter, and up in the summer, by one or two degrees. Turn the air conditioning and heat back a few degrees when you leave for work. You can add a setback thermostat if you are away for long periods each day. Also set back the thermostat at night a few degrees. For every degree you lower the thermostat, you can save three percent on your heating bill. When cooling, changing the thermostat from 70 to 75 degrees could save as much as 25 percent. For each degree over 70, you could save 3-5 percent.

➤ When it is very hot outside you should turn the air conditioning up a few degrees and supplement it with a room, or ceiling, fan. A fan is a lot less expensive to operate.

➤ If you have an older central air conditioner or heating system, consider upgrading to a newer, more efficient model with a high efficiency rating. (The higher the number the more efficient the unit is.) You could save thirty-five percent or more on your bill.

➤ Many of us are ready to buy new rugs, curtains, and furniture when they get stained or dirty. I have found that there are some excellent products that can make those items look new again. The only problem is that you usually need to clean the entire sofa, or all of the curtains, because when you clean just one area the rest suddenly looks dirty. No matter what product you use, you should always test it first on an area that cannot be seen in case it discolors or damages the fabric. I have used one such product that works great for many items. It is called Oxi Clean and I will swear by this product. My wife had dried coffee stains on her car's floor mat and seat that I could not wash off. I sprayed the areas with Oxi Clean once or twice and the stains disappeared right before my eyes without scrubbing. Another product that works well on calcium, lime, and rust stains is CLR. In all cases, follow the manufacturers' recommendations for using the products.

➢ Have your electric utility company install an *OP meter* (off-peak hour meter) or enroll in an off-hour rate program. Use high-powered equipment during those hours (washer, dryer). The appliances you connect to this service are on a timer and can only operate during certain times of the day. An electrician is needed to separate the electrical circuits. The electric company will usually charge less than half price for the use of the appliances that are connected to the off-peak hour meter. That is a substantial savings. Check with your electrical supplier for rates and determine if this service is for you.

➢ Make certain your washing machine, dryer, and dishwasher are full before using. Use lower temperature water for your washing machine cycles. Consider using shorter cycles. Always clean the dryer air filter before you use it. Do not rinse your dishes before putting them in the dishwasher. Let dishes dry by themselves. If your dishwasher does not have an air-dry switch, turn the unit off after the rinse cycle. Open the door to allow air to circulate.

➢ Change the air filter regularly in heating and air conditioning systems. A blocked air filter makes the system work harder and keeps it from running efficiently. Changing the filter regularly can save you 5 percent on your energy bill.

➢ Select lighter color paints for your rooms. Darker colors require more lighting to illuminate the room.

➢ We have all bought new items that work fine for a year or so. Then you look for the owner's manual and cannot find it. In most cases you no longer have to spend money calling the manufacturer to order a new owner's manual. Today you are able to retrieve most manuals online.

Continue to keep owner's manuals, however, because you never know when the company might go out of business or cannot be found online.

➤ Lower your water heater thermostat to 122 degrees F, or less. For every 10 degrees you lower it, you will save 3-5 percent. You also avoid accidental burns.

➤ Insulate the water heater with a thick insulation cover. This can save you 5-9 percent on the use of this appliance. Also insulate the hot water pipes.

➤ Drain a gallon of water from the hot water heater every 6 months. This will help extend the life of the unit and helps it run more efficiently by removing sediment from the bottom of the tank.

➤ Do not assume that when an item is not working or is broken that you need to replace it. It may only need a simple fix.

➤ Keeping your freezer full helps to keep items cold, but do not over-pack it because the air needs to circulate around the food. For times when the freezer is half-empty, use old plastic containers (milk container, soda bottle, etc.), filled with water, to take up the extra space.

➤ Vacuum refrigerator coils at least twice a year. Follow the manufacturer's recommendations for cleaning.

➤ Before considering renovations or adding an addition to your home, check with your local township to see if you need any permits. If you install new AC circuits that lead to a fire, and you did not have the proper permits, you may not be covered by your insurance company. If you install a wall or a shed that does not have a permit, the township can make you take it down.

➢ If you cook with an electric stove, turn off the burner a few minutes before you would normally turn it off. It will remain hot and continue to cook for another three to five minutes. Cover your pots with lids to minimize heat loss.

➢ If you are going away for more than a few days, unplug devices that consume power, turn down your water heater, and shut off the main water valve. Do not unplug critical devices (sump pump, alarm system, etc.).

➢ Be prepared to pay your real-estate taxes early and save by paying the discounted rate. This can save you hundreds of dollars per year.

➢ Do not buy a room air conditioner that is designed for a larger room than you need to cool. It will run less efficiently than one that is the proper size. The properly sized air conditioners are designed to run longer, which helps remove moisture and humidity from the air. A larger unit than you need will turn off and on more frequently, and will not maintain a constant temperature.

➢ Take a shower instead of a bath. You will save on water and utilities. When taking a bath, cut back on some of the water used, do not fill the tub to the top. A bath uses 50 to 60 gallons of water. An older showerhead, without any water saver features, uses 4-6 gallons of water per minute. If the showerhead has a water saver, it may only use 2 gallons per minute.

➢ Some items have lifetime warranties. Instead of throwing them out when they are broken, contact the manufacturer. They will either fix or replace the item. I can think of at least two brands that most of us are very familiar with, Totes and Craftsman.

➢ Hang clothes on an outside line instead of using your dryer.

➤ Buy yourself a "how to fix all items in and around your house" book. It will surely pay for itself in the long run. They also make great housewarming presents. That is, of course, if they already have my book.

➤ Take advantage of daylight by opening curtains or blinds and allowing light to enter the room. Remember, however, to shield the excess heat in the summer months, to save on air conditioning bills. Make use of the sun's heat in the winter by keeping the blinds open.

➤ Do you have a favorite CD player, stereo or portable TV that uses and drains batteries regularly? Consider buying two sets of rechargeable batteries. They will not last as long between charges, but who cares if you no longer have to spend money on batteries. (Rechargeable batteries can usually be recharged three to six hundred times. It depends on what you are using them to power. Let them drain all the way down before recharging.)

➤ We tend to stick to name brands when purchasing batteries. There are many alternatives when it comes to buying alkaline, heavy duty, and standard batteries. Consider buying store brand batteries. They usually last about the same as name brands, and they are much cheaper. Always look for packs of 7 to 12, depending on the battery, to get the best deals. Store them in a cool place.

➤ Ask your local phone company to look at your past bills and call patterns. Inquire if there is a better plan for you that could save you money. Check into your plan's options. If you make many long distance calls, there are carrier companies that offer packages that include some of your local phone features, plus unlimited long distance within the United States. If you have a cell phone, it may be cheaper to use that for long distance calls. Consider using the Internet if available to you. In some cases you can take advantage of free video and audio conferencing.

➢ Rather than paying a monthly fee to a long distance carrier company, it may be cheaper to dial an access code when making long distance calls. Check the rates. Consider purchasing an inexpensive prepaid calling card.

➢ The deed on your house (also referred to as "title") is your official proof that you are the owner of the land and property. Your mortgage company usually holds on to the deed until your loan is paid off. Make certain the deed is sent to you once the loan is paid in full.

➢ Turn on unused faucets in your home at least once every two months. This will prevent sewer gas and odor from entering your home. You only need to let the water run for 15 seconds, or until the trap fills up. Water in the trap (the "U" shaped area of the pipe) acts to block the gas and odor. Once the water evaporates from lack of use, this function is lost. Depending on your region and the location of drain in your home, this can occur as early as 2 weeks from last use.

➢ Do you have a drawer or door that seems to stick and will not slide in or out freely? Just slide a bar of soap along the track and any other locations that may be rubbing. Work the drawer or door back and forth a few times.

➢ Make your house more energy-efficient. Fix air duct leaks, window and door leaks, add insulation where needed- attic, garage, door strips, etc. You can reuse the white foam packing from meat trays under your outlet and switch plates to prevent drafts. Just wash them, allow to dry, and cut them to fit.

➢ If you are planning to move, consider taking any items that can be reused at your new location, such as chandeliers, draperies, fancy fixtures, fluorescent bulbs, etc. Yes, I said fluorescent bulbs. They usually cost anywhere from $4.00 to $10.00 apiece, while a regular

bulb costs only about fifty cents each. It is worth your
time to make the exchange. Same with curtains, if the
windows at the new location are the same size. If the
windows are smaller, the curtains can be tailored to fit.
They could also be used in a different room. I have known
too many people that throw things away when they move,
and regret it later when they discover how expensive those
items are to replace. I am not telling you to be a pack rat,
but just to give it some serious thought before you throw
things away.

➢ Always use cold water when possible. This will cut down
on the use of the hot water heater. (If you have a single
lever faucet, lift the lever up and to the right for cold
water. If you are just lifting straight up, you are still using
hot water.)

➢ Repair minor water leaks (faucets, toilets, outdoor hoses,
instant hot water dispensers, etc.). The water wasted adds
up faster than you think. If you have a faucet that drips a
drop every second, it wastes more than 2200 gallons of
water in a year.

Shopping

➢ If you have a large family, consider buying some items in
bulk (vitamins, dry goods, etc.). Do not buy quantities that
will not be consumed before their expiration date.

➢ You can often find perishable items marked down (deli,
donuts, bread, rolls, etc.) at the grocery store or
supermarket, one hour before closing. Talk to the manager
of the department if an item is not already discounted, and
it is about to expire. Ask him/her what the policy is so you
know what to look for. Once they get to know you, you
may get deals that are not available to the public. The
prices are usually adjusted with a marker. Make sure you
let the cashier know before he/she scans the item or rings

it up. Since vegetables and fruits have no expiration date, you need to look for signs of aging. You can often get major discounts on those items. Sometimes they may even give them to you at no charge.

➢ Look for coupons in your local paper, on the Internet, and in magazines before grocery shopping. Apply for supermarket member cards that give discounts on store specials. Use a credit card that gives you cash back when paying for your purchases.

➢ If you shop regularly in a particular store, consider obtaining their store credit card. Many stores send out special discounts, incentives, coupons and gifts to their credit card customers, even if you never use it.

➢ Below is a list of Web sites that can help you with coupons, rebates, discounts, and even some free samples.
www.currentcodes.com   www.dealcatcher.com
www.coolsavings.com   www.edealfinder.com

➢ If you are shopping with your spouse who keeps buying and buying, let him/her carry the bags. This will keep him/her aware of how many items have already been purchased.

➢ When looking to buy an item, consider last year's model, a scratch or dent model, or a discontinued, demo or floor model. If the item is an electrical or mechanical device, make sure it comes with a full warranty.

➢ Consider shopping for clothing at large outlet centers. The best bargains are usually in the back of the store. Do not take any sale signs or discounts at face value. You should have an idea what the item normally costs to know if you are really getting a good deal.

➢ Clip coupons for products you buy at the grocery store. Many stores will double or even triple the coupon value at certain times. They do usually have a limit on what they will pay.

➢ Every so often department stores hold sales offering 20% off everything in the store. If the store allows, consider purchasing a gift card at this time. A $100.00 gift card will only cost you $80.00 and can be used in the future. Now you can wait for their next big sale and use your gift card to compound your savings even more.

➢ Some gift cards (or gift certificates) expire if not used by a certain date; others start to lose value monthly after a certain date (usually 1 year or more from the date purchased). Do not let this happen to you. If you have a $50.00 gift card that is about to expire, take it to the store and purchase two new gift cards for $25.00 each. Tell the store personnel you are buying them as gifts for others. Many store clerks do not seem to be familiar with this process. You may need to get the store manager involved. If you need further help see Chapter 3 on Customer Service Issues.

➢ Mini markets, delis, and convenience stores are conveniently situated, but their prices are usually higher.

➢ Think twice before buying an extended warranty for a product you have purchased. Most of the time they are a waste of money. The extended warranty may be helpful if you feel the product is at risk of breaking because of the way it will be used, or because of the environment it will be used in. In my case, most items break just after the warranty expires.

➢ Have you bought food and later found out that something was wrong with it (fish smelled or tasted fishy, meat was extremely grisly, item was out of date, or the fruit was rotten inside). Call the store and let them know. As long as you have a receipt, they will give you your money back the next time you are in the store.

- For those of you who have a computer, think twice before buying software, games, and utilities and application programs. Many companies on the Internet offer free software that may fit your needs. They may not be the latest version, but when it is free, you cannot complain.

- Some supermarkets accept other supermarkets' coupons. Most of the larger chains offer a card that keeps track of your spending habits. That same card also gives you credit for items that have store coupons or discounts just by presenting the card at checkout. Be sure to get cards for all the stores at which you shop even the stores you do not visit regularly. When you do go, you do not want to miss the discounts.

- I have learned that it is not always in your best interest to renew contracts or subscriptions early or on time. Do not get me wrong I am not saying to pay critical items such as HMO bills or insurance bills late. What I am saying is to take a gamble on items that are not going to have an impact on your daily life or credit report. We all get those constant reminders to renew your lawn service contract, CD or book club membership, magazine subscription, or your oil heating repair contract. I have found that most companies offer you additional incentives and discounts if they think you are not planning to renew. They start in the last few weeks and the offers get better about one month after the expiration.

  I am not saying to gamble with your heating repair contract if it ends in the middle of winter. However, if it ends in April you will probably not be at much of a risk. You could always do without a magazine or CD for a month. In fact, many times they will rush out your first order so you are not far behind. I have seen as much as thirty-five percent savings from lawn companies. If you actually cancel contracts and switch to a new company, they will usually contact you the following season and offer you a better deal just to get you back.

➢ Do not be fooled by companies that sell the same product in different sized containers. They often lead you to believe that the larger sized container has a larger amount of product, which may not be true. They may even add comments like "new and improved" or "30 percent more." Be sure you check the total content or weight information. Packaging can be very deceptive. Always check the unit price (price per pound, quart, etc.) when comparing different sized containers. Most people assume the larger size is always the better deal. Sometimes, however, it is cheaper to buy two smaller sized containers and still receive the same amount of product, or more, but at a lower unit price.

➢ Unless you are one of those thrifty consumers who only purchase items when they are on sale, I would recommend you only go shopping when you truly need an item. Too many of us browse the stores, malls, outlet centers, specialty shops, etc., and before we know it, we have spent a few hundred dollars on items we did not plan to buy in the first place.

➢ Many items can be purchased at your local dollar store. The products vary from one store to another but generally include cleaning products, cereals, hardware, paper products, groceries, beauty supplies, and more.

➢ Make sure you send in rebates. That is tax-free money being returned to you, and it adds up over time.

➢ If you are considering buying expensive furniture, or multiple rooms of furniture, you should check Web sites of companies located in North Carolina. You can get some great deals on furniture from those locations even with the shipping and delivery charges added in. You could also use their prices for bargaining power with your local furniture dealer. You could save hundreds, even thousands, towards the purchase of new furniture.

➤ Do not be fooled when companies "guarantee the lowest price." This only means it is the "lowest published price."

➤ When you buy certain items pay attention to the warranty. It may be worth spending a few dollars more for an item that comes with a full warranty. However, do not be fooled by the term "lifetime warranty." Many of these warranties have a time limit. You need to read the fine print. As long as it is explained in the fine print, companies are allowed to use these deceptions. Lifetime <u>guarantees</u> may not be deceptive, but read the fine print. In some cases the guarantee refers to the actual life of the product, which is determined by the manufacturer. There are two types of warranties - full and limited.

> A full warranty needs to meet standards set by the federal government. It covers the person who owns the product. There is no time limit to the implied warranty. The warranty service must be provided free of charge. If the item cannot be repaired, they must give you a replacement or refund your money.

> A limited warranty allows you to have the defective item repaired or replaced within a specified period.

There is also what is known as implied warranties, such as the "warranty of merchantability." All this warranty means is that the seller promises the product will do what it is supposed to do. For example, a car will run and a knife will cut. There are a few more implied warranties created by state laws.

If your purchase does not come with a written warranty, it is still covered by an implied warranty. This is true unless the product is marked "as is," or the seller indicates, in writing, that no warranty is given. Implied warranty coverage can last as long as four years, although the length of the coverage varies from state to state. Your state consumer protection office can provide more information about implied warranty coverage in your state.

➤ Create a shopping list and try to stick to the list. If you are hungry when you go food shopping, you are likely to buy extra items. If you wear glasses, take them with you so you can compare prices.

➤ Many items are seasonal or go on sale once a year. If possible, delay your purchase until then. Some examples are white sales for sheets and towels in January, sales for small household items after Christmas, school supplies from late July to early September, winter clothes in February and March, tools around late May to early June, etc. Not to mention that many of these items are on sale around Christmastime or other major holidays. Just ask your local store when the items you are looking for tend to go on sale.

➤ Shopping for major appliances can be very confusing. Some have many different features that you need to compare. The prices tend to be all over the place. Remember that most of these prices are negotiable. Use the techniques outlined in this book to get the best price.

Look through consumer magazines and check the repair records for the different manufacturers. Be wary of manufacturers who imply that their appliances do not break as often. Do your own research and you might be surprised. I can think of one company out there who would like us to believe that they have a great track record. If you research that company in consumer results, they are probably one of the worst. They even had me fooled at one time.

Most large appliances have some type of system that rates the efficiency of the product. Below are the ratings that you should look for when shopping. Always look for energy efficient appliances.

> Clothes washers, dishwashers, and hot water heaters are measured by EF (*Energy Factor*) rating. The higher the number the less it will cost you to operate the product. Washers and dryers are starting to be measured by the MEF (*Modified Energy Factor*). It is based on EF and any remaining moisture. The higher the number the less it will cost you to operate.
> Water heaters also have FHR (First Hour Rating). This tells you how much hot water can be produced in the first hour from a cold start. The higher the number the better.
>
> Central air conditioners and central heat pumps are rated by SEER (*Seasonal Energy Efficiency Rating*). The higher the number the less power it uses. Central air-to-air units with heat pumps are also rated by HSPF (*Heating Seasonal Performance Factor*). The higher the number the better.
>
> Oil systems, natural gas and electric furnace systems are rated by the AFUE (*Annual Fuel Utilization Efficiency*). The higher the number the more efficient the system is.

Use the table on page 173, to get an estimate of what your savings could be with a new high efficiency system. The table lists approximate annual operating costs for units with various SEER Ratings. For example, if your current air conditioner has a SEER of 6.0 and your annual operating cost is $600, the cost to operate a new 14 SEER system will be approximately $260, giving you an annual savings of about $340, or 57 percent!

Cooling Efficiency - SEER Rating											
6.0	7.0	8.0	9.0	10.0	11.0	12.0	13.0	14.0	15.0	16.0	17.0
$200	$175	$150	$135	$120	$110	$100	$90	$85	$80	$75	$70
$300	260	225	200	180	165	150	135	130	120	115	105
$400	345	300	270	240	220	200	185	170	160	150	140
$500	430	375	335	300	275	250	230	215	200	190	175
$600	515	450	400	360	330	300	280	260	240	225	210
$700	600	525	465	420	385	350	325	300	280	265	250
$800	690	605	540	485	440	405	370	345	320	300	285
$900	780	685	610	550	500	455	415	385	360	340	320
Approximate Annual Operating Cost											

Use the table below to get an estimated cost savings by replacing an old furnace with a high efficiency model. If your current furnace is more than 10 years old, the efficiency is likely to be about 60%. For example, if your current furnace is 60% efficient and your annual operating cost is $700, the cost to operate a new 93% AFUE system will be between $425 and $450, giving you an annual savings of approximately $250, or about 36 percent!

Heating Efficiency - AFUE Rating						
60%	65%	70%	75%	80%	90%	95%
$400	$365	$340	$315	$295	$255	$240
$500	460	425	395	365	320	305
$600	550	510	470	440	385	365
$700	640	595	550	515	450	425
$800	735	675	630	585	515	485
$900	825	760	710	660	580	545
$1000	915	845	785	735	640	605
Approximate Annual Operating Cost						

Freezers and refrigerators have an Energy Guide label that shows how many kWh (*kilowatt-hours*) the model will consume in electricity within one year. The lower the number the cheaper it will be to operate.

Room air conditioners are rated by the EER (*Energy Efficiency Rating*). Higher numbered units cost less to operate.

Another rating used is the Energy Star label. This label is also placed on small and large appliances to identify that they are energy efficient products. Energy Star labeled appliances exceed the existing federal efficiency standards.

All of these rating systems were created by the Federal Government, U.S. Department of Energy, and U.S Environmental Protection Agency in order to help consumers select products that will save them on operating cost related to utilities cost. It does not take into account the item's mechanical repair history.

You could also contact your local utility and/or energy organization for information about high-efficiency products and rebate programs. These programs sometimes offer cash incentives, tax credits, or financing for buying certain products. The rebate programs vary from region to region. The following site may be helpful for choosing your next appliance. This site has many good links and information but does not deal or respond to public request.

www.cee1.org

The best single resource for this type of information can be found at this Web site. It has qualifying product lists, manufacturer lists, and can help consumers locate these products.

www.energystar.gov

Chapter 8

Travel

➢ When traveling, use your work address on luggage tags. The airlines can still contact you if your luggage is misplaced, but burglars will not have access to your home address while you are on vacation and your house is empty.

➢ If you plan to stay in hotels, you really want to do your homework. Rates vary from one hotel to another. In fact, they vary a lot within the same hotel. The rack rate is usually the most expensive rate. Ask if they have any specials, packages, or promotional rates. Always tell them the rates are too high and ask what other options they have available. Ask them for their lowest, or rock bottom rate.

➢ If there is an extended flight delay due to the fault of the airline (not weather related), insist the airline provide meals and hotel accommodations, as needed, during the delay.

➢ When traveling around holidays, get to the airport early (at least 2 ½ hours before domestic flights and 3 ½ hours before international flights).

➢ Ask for a seat in an exit row. These rows are usually much roomier. You must be 14 or older to sit there.

➢ If you are going to a convention or visiting a particular location, they may have special rates in place. If you are a member of an automobile club, travel club, or affiliated with a corporation, you may be eligible for a discount. These discounts are not necessarily lower than their normal rack rates. Sometimes these discounted rates provide upgraded rooms. Always ask if they have anything cheaper. If you already made reservations and find a better rate somewhere else, let them know. They may lower their rate or throw in other incentives to keep you from canceling the reservation.

Calling the hotel directly can save you even more because they sometimes offer unadvertised specials. Speak to someone that has the authority to negotiate. If possible, stay away from hotels that are right where the main attractions are located. Staying a few blocks away can save you money on the hotel and food purchases. Often, the hotels and restaurants in the center of it all are tourist traps.

➤ Some businesses such as casinos, new hotels, new restaurants, time-shares, and businesses in remote locations offer better deals hoping to attract you as a customer. (Sometimes you may have to listen to a few hours of presentations.)

➤ After arriving at the hotel, start your second round of negotiating. See if they can upgrade your room (better view, late checkout, or upgrade to larger room or suite).

➤ Carry film with you, not in your checked luggage. X-ray machines may damage undeveloped film. Most security personnel will hand search if requested.

➤ When flying at night, consider bringing earplugs with you to block out the engine noise if you want to be able to sleep during the flight.

➤ When traveling with a group, or with children, always have a plan in place in case you are separated. Before your trip, select a meeting location. Everyone on the trip should have the name, address, and phone number of the place where you are staying.

➤ You could always save money by carrying your own luggage. Many hotels provide luggage carts that make the job easier. This also ensures that your luggage is not damaged, and there are no worries about something turning up missing.

➢ Do not accept a kindly person's offer to take your picture with your camera. It could be a scam and he/she will run off with your camera once you give it to them. Always select the person yourself.

➢ Many airlines charge for headphones to plug into the audio system for TV, movies and radio. If you travel frequently, consider buying headphones with universal plugs. Sometimes you can even use the headphones from your portable tape or compact disc player.

➢ Be careful when you buy jewelry and art work outside of your local area. There are many dishonest people out there. If you make a jewelry purchase and are told the item weighs thirty-five grams and is 18 *karat* gold, go to another jeweler nearby and have them weigh it to confirm this information. If it was an expensive item, you may also want to have it tested for the amount of gold used in the jewelry. There is usually a small cost to do this type of testing.

➢ If you travel to a country that uses a different currency, always be sure of which currency rate is being used when they are quoting prices. Tell the person you are dealing with that you want to clarify this so neither of you gets confused. This Web site has a currency converter so you can figure out your exchange rate. All currency rates are updated regularly.

www.xe.com

➢ When traveling, carry a variety of snacks with you so you do not have to pay the higher prices in the hotel or at convenience stores. If you need to make purchases, stop at a supermarket. Take things back to your room if you are staying for a few days.

- When traveling, consider alternative routes to reach your destination. Instead of flying to the planned airport, a flight to a nearby airport may be less expensive. From there, take an inexpensive commuter flight, train, bus or even a rental car to your destination. This can easily save you hundreds of dollars.

- Use credit cards for purchases in other countries when possible. This will ensure that you get the best exchange rate for your money.

- Airfares change regularly so be sure to check with your airline frequently.

- When traveling keep your valuables with you at all times. Keep half of your money and credit cards in one place, and the rest with you in a different location, just in case you are pick-pocketed or your bag is stolen.

- Try not to use local stores for exchanging money because they will often give you a lower exchange rate. Some locations, like casinos and shopping malls, offer a higher exchange rate without any conversion fees. They do this to attract new customers. Take advantage of these places when converting your money.

- Always ask the travel agent or airline if they know of any promotions that are coming up. If they do, ask them if they can hold it for you, or when you can call back for the discount. Sometimes they will let you put a hold on it for a few days. If you can wait the few days, you will be able to take advantage of the promotional offer.

- Teach your children to memorize your home phone number (including area code) and that of at least one other relative.

➤ Always call the airline before leaving home to confirm your flight. Do the same thing before returning.

➤ When checking in your bags, tell them that they contain fragile items. They will usually label them "fragile." The bags will be treated with more care and will most likely be one of the first to appear at pick up.

➤ Most hotels have an area with coupons and pamphlets for local attractions and restaurants. Many times they keep maps of the area behind the service counter and will provide them for free if you ask.

➤ Look for cheap calling cards if you need to make phone calls from pay phones. Some cards offer $.035 cents or less per minute for calls within the US. Consider taking the phone card with you when traveling. Make calls from a pay phone outside of the hotel. Many hotels have high surcharges for using their phones. Some even charge fees for dialing toll-free numbers.

➤ Request a confirmation number when making reservations to ensure that your request is reserved. Ask them if your entire request is guaranteed. If you change your mind and cancel the reservation, be sure you get a separate confirmation number for the cancellation. You may need this number to prove that you canceled the reservation. Many hotels will charge you for one day if you do not arrive on the scheduled arrival date.

➤ Many credit card companies offer accidental life insurance for free if you use their card to purchase the airline ticket or other form of travel.

➤ Always double check your reservations to make certain there are no mistakes in the price, arrival and departure dates, package deals and limitations, type of beds requested, smoking or non-smoking rooms, etc.

➤ If you are planning to travel and have a specific destination in mind, start looking around three to four months ahead of time. This will help you get better deals. If you want to travel but have no particular preference of location, you could call a last minute travel company. They usually offer some fantastic deals. The closer to your departure date when you book, the better the deal will be. Look for places that include meals or have meal plans.

➤ Find out where the local folks eat. Do not get caught in the tourist traps.

➤ Join each airline's frequent flyer program when you fly. Also join the hotel frequent guest programs.

➤ After getting the best deal from the travel agent, call the airline for a quote to make sure the price you have is better.

➤ Do the reverse of what others do. Travel during off-peak seasons. When flying, consider flights that leave in the afternoon, mid-week or at night. Take flights that make one stop on the way. Be flexible with your departure date and airline. Consider going to a country that offers a higher exchange rate for your existing currency. You could save as much as 50 percent with some exchange rates.

➤ Using an airline that offers electronic ticketing will usually save you money. You will be ticketless and it may be easier to transfer to another airline if your flight should be canceled.

➤ When buying airline tickets in advance (7, 14, 21, 45, 90 days) ask about their Advance Purchase Excursion (APEX). These can lower the cost of regular rates by one third or more. These tickets are usually nonrefundable and may require staying over Saturday.

➤ Many flights are very expensive if they do not include a Saturday night stay. Instead of buying one round trip ticket to your destination, it may actually be cheaper to buy two round trip tickets. Each should have a Saturday stay over. You will only use one ticket from each round trip. One ticket should originate in your departure city. The other should originate in your destination city. Some airlines do not allow you to use this method so I suggest buying your tickets from two different airlines. Sometimes it may even be cheaper to buy both of your round trip tickets from the destination city.

Example: You want to travel from Philadelphia to Chicago. You will be departing on Monday and returning on Thursday, 3 days later. Buy a round trip ticket from Philadelphia to depart Monday and return Sunday. Buy a second round trip ticket to depart Chicago Thursday and return Sunday. When you leave Philadelphia, use the first half of ticket one. When you leave Chicago, use the first half of ticket two. You will simply discard the remaining tickets, but can save hundreds of dollars by doing this.

➤ Buy your tickets through a consolidator. Consolidators buy large blocks of airline seats at substantial discounts. They then resell those tickets to travel agents, last minute discounters, and the public. You can sometimes save over 50% off the lowest priced tickets. When you use a consolidator, you have certain restrictions and will probably not qualify for frequent flyer miles. The seats must be sold by certain dates.

➤ Chew gum during take-off to reduce pressure in your ears.

➤ Make sure that all gifts are unwrapped, as security will need to check the contents.

➤ Many people are confused when it comes to tipping others for services provided. What should you give the taxi driver after you arrive at your destination? These things happen to us all the time when you are served dinner, the bartender serves you a drink, or the bellhop carries your luggage to your room. How much should you pay for these services? I will give you some guidelines. Again, they are only guidelines and should depend on the quality of service received.

Hotel bellhop	$1 - 2 for each piece of luggage
Hotel concierge	$1 - 3 for quick help & information $5 for detailed information and setting up reservations
Hotel maid	$1 - 2 per day, after 2 nights, usually given at end of stay. $5 - 10 per week
Door keeper	$1 - 2 for hailing a cab
Baggage handler	$1 per bag
Skycap	$1 per bag
Bartender	10% - 15% of the bar bill
Waiter/waitress	15% - 20% of the bill
Coat check	$1 for one or two coats
Aestheticians	$1.50 per treatment
Barber/hairdresser	15% of the bill but not less than $1. You do not have to tip the owner.
Manicurist	$1 - 2
Shampooer	$1 minimum
Home delivery	$2 - 5
Massage therapist	15% - 20% of bill
Gas station attendants	rarely over $.50 cents
Parking valet	$1 - 2
Taxi driver	10% - 15% of the fare, but not less than $1
Limousine driver	15% - 20% of bill
Tour bus driver	$1 minimum up to 15% if over $10.00
Tour guide	$.50 cent per person, and $1 if they guide you all day
Maître d'	$5 - 10
Movers	8% - 10% of bill
Usher at sports arena	$.50 cents to $1 per group
Shoe shiner	$.50 cents minimum
Wine steward	$3 minimum or 10% of bill

If you are on a cruise, use the following guidelines. The gratuities are usually paid at the end. On some cruise lines, tips are already included.

Waiter	$3 per person per day
Assistant waiter/ Busboy	$1.50 per person per day
Cabin steward/ess	$3 per person per day
Chief housekeeper	$5 per person per cruise, up to 11 nights, $7.50 for 14 nights, $8.50 for 17 nights
Restaurant manager	$7.50 per person up to 11 nights, $9 up to 14 nights, $12 for 17 nights
Maître d' & head waiter	Tip at your discretion
Butler (suites only)	$3 per person per day
Bar bill	15% is usually added automatically

Most staff on cruises makes less than minimum wage and work more than 15 hours per day.

Tipping should not prevent you from going out to dinner. If you do not have the capability to give a fifteen - percent tip, then go out and give them what you can afford. Be sure to let the waiter or waitress know that the service was very good if it was.

Some hotels and restaurants include the tip in your bill. For groups of six or more the tip is usually included. Many times the tip is based on eighteen percent. If you do not feel comfortable with that percentage let them know what you are willing to pay. If the service was poor, make sure you deduct from the percentage. If the service was exceptional, you may want to add one or two percent. Remember, a tip is something you are providing for good service. It is not an obligation.

Do not tip salespeople, public transportation bus drivers, theater ushers, museum guides, hotel clerks, doctors, teachers, or employees of fast food restaurants. Tipping government employees, police officers, government officials, or judges could be interpreted as a bribe, which is illegal. It is not necessary to tip the owner of a barbershop, beauty shop, coffee shop, or any other business owner. It is up to you but the owner often charges a higher price for his/her services than the people that work for them.

Do not forget to consider an extra tip around the holidays for those who serve you regularly (mail carrier, baby sitters, newspaper delivery person, trash hauler, maid, haircutter, etc.).

> Full time baby sitter 1 - 2 weeks pay, newspaper boy $10 - 20, maid 1 - 2 weeks pay, mail carrier $5 - 20.

Always calculate your tip based on what the bill would be if you were not using coupons or other discounts. Do not include the taxes in your tip calculations.

Below is a tip chart based on 15% and 20% tipping.

Amount	15%	20%	Amount	15%	20%
$1.00	$ .15	$ .20	$10.00	$ 1.50	$ 2.00
$2.00	$ .30	$ .40	$20.00	$ 3.00	$ 4.00
$3.00	$ .45	$ .60	$30.00	$ 4.50	$ 6.00
$4.00	$ .60	$ .80	$40.00	$ 6.00	$ 8.00
$5.00	$ .75	$ 1.00	$50.00	$ 7.50	$10.00
$6.00	$ .90	$ 1.20	$60.00	$ 9.00	$12.00
$7.00	$1.05	$ 1.40	$70.00	$10.50	$14.00
$8.00	$1.20	$ 1.60	$80.00	$12.00	$16.00
$9.00	$1.35	$ 1.80	$90.00	$13.50	$18.00

If you do not have your tip chart handy, you can use my formula for figuring out the tip. If your bill comes out to $78.00, I will show you how you can easily calculate the tip at 10, 15, and 20 percent. Just follow the simple steps. To make it easier you can round out the cost of the bill to the nearest dollar.

1. For 10 percent of $78.00, just move the decimal point one over to the left and drop the last number. $7.80 is 10% of the bill.

2. To figure out 15%, do the previous step and divide $7.80 by 2, which is $3.90. Now add $7.80 and $3.90 together to get $11.70. $11.70 is 15% of your bill ($78.00).

3. To figure out 20% just perform step one and double the number. $15.60 is 20% of your bill ($78.00).

➤   Take advantage of online flight check-in if available. Only about 5% of people use it. It saves you from standing in a long line at the airport as you can check in and print your boarding passes at home. You can usually do it within 24 hours of your flight time.

➤   Ask for a hand search of homeopathic medicines or supplements containing enzymes. Do not put them through the x-ray machines.

Internet Searches

The Internet is a very powerful and useful tool. It allows you to find information on just about any topic. It can be used to comparative shop, educate, locate businesses, learn how to do something, locate people, find specialty hard to find items, and many other things. Sometimes it may seem a bit overwhelming when it provides more information than you need. When these issues occur, just be patient and redefine your search criteria. You may need to eliminate some words or text. The following is a brief lesson on using the Internet to your advantage, and an overview of commands that may make searching easier for you.

To conduct a good search, it is important to use a good search engine. I have found that some search engines work better for me than others do. I cannot stress enough the importance of using multiple search engines because they do not all find the same information. Sometimes I can search five different engines and come up empty. Then, the sixth search reveals pages of information. Each search engine contains some type of help screen that explains how to enter your search criteria in order to obtain the best match for the information you are looking for. Many search engines also offer an advanced search menu, which provides even more ways to conduct your search.

I will start by giving you an example of things that I am trying to accomplish. I will then explain different ways to conduct searches. Just remember that there is no perfect way to perform a search. Part of it is skill, the rest is luck. It is also possible to receive different results for the same search, at different times.

Example 1
You are interested in a car that you saw on the street, but all you know about it is that it is a Toyota.

When searching for a specific company, you should first try to type the company's name followed by ".com" on the command line of your browser menu. "www.toyota.com".
If that does not work, click on the word "search" on the screen. Type in the word "toyota" at the prompt. You will get many results back for that search criteria. Look over the results until you find something that resembles the information you are trying to find. In this case you would look for something that refers to the main company "Toyota Motor Corporation." Sometimes you will see something that says "official company site" on the first page or two of the information received. Click on the underlined heading of the site you wish to view. If you want to choose a different site, click on the word "Back," at the top of the screen, until you are back to the results page.

Once you find the correct Toyota site, click on an option, such as "models" to locate the vehicle you were interested in. You will also be able to see the options available on this vehicle as well as other information just by clicking through the various menus at this site. (This is not an exact representation of this site but just an idea of what it may be like to locate the vehicle.) Most sites have some similarities and are fairly easy to navigate from the home page (this is usually the first page you arrive at).

I will now assume you would like further information on the 2003 Toyota Corolla. You can check out the Web site listed in the "Helpful Hints / Comments" section of Chapter 2, or you can conduct a new search to find other sites that have information on that vehicle.

Return to the search menu and type "Toyota Corolla 2003" at the prompt. To refine your search and cut down on the amount of responses you receive, add words to your search topic. For example, if you would like to know what type of reviews the car might have received type in "Toyota Corolla 2003 review." This will return fewer responses, but more should be better related to your subject. If you wanted to find out if the car was redesigned you might do a search on "Toyota Corolla 2003 redesigned." Let us say that you were hoping it was a sporty looking car. You can now expand your search to include those words "Toyota Corolla 2003 redesign sporty look." The more words you use the more specific your search results will be. Your search results may be listed in the order of closest matched results to your least matched results. Sometimes you need to change words you select or use fewer words to get the information you are searching for.

Example 2
You want to find out about things that are happening in your area. You could just enter your zip code or city in the search window. Using both will give you a better result.

Example 3
You are planning a trip to Philadelphia, Pennsylvania and would like to stay in center city. You would like to know what hotels are in the area. You may do a search on the following: "Philadelphia center city" or "Philadelphia hotels center city." If you are looking for something cheap, you may add one of these words to your search criteria to locate a better deal: cheap, discount, special, bargain, lowest, deal. This does not mean they are the only hotels that have good deals but they are the only ones your specified

search criteria found. The key to finding what you want is to keep refining your search criteria.

Example 4
You want to find a recipe for chicken divan. Type in "chicken divan" at the search prompt and you have the answer.

Example 5
Your refrigerator breaks and you need to replace a part. Enter the "make" and "model" number in the search window and in seconds you have many companies that sell parts for that refrigerator. You can even shop around once you know the "part model number" by doing a search on that. You can even obtain owner's manuals that you may have misplaced at many manufacturers' web sites.

The following information is for those of you already comfortable with simple searches. There are words called operators, or terms, that can help you in conducting searches. Knowing some of these commands can make searching easier. Each search engine has its own words and formats. You should familiarize yourself with commands the first time you use a new search engine. Below are examples of how some of these commands may be used. I will refer to the Toyota Corolla 2003 for my search criteria.

Toyota **OR** Corolla - use of "OR" or "|" (vertical line in front of the word) in your search will give you results of either Toyota or Corolla in any article, or even articles that contain both names.

Toyota **AND** Corolla - use of the "AND" or "+" (plus sign in front of the word) or "&" (ampersand in between words) will only give you results of articles that contain both Toyota and Corolla in the same article.

Toyota **NOT** Sporty - use of the "NOT" or "-" (minus sign in front of the word) or "!" (exclamation point in front of the word) will give you all articles that contain Toyota only if it also does not contain sporty.

Toyota **NEAR** Corolla - use of the "NEAR" or "~" (italic tilde) will only show up if both Toyota and Corolla are near each other in the article. If the words are far apart from each other, it will not show up in your search results. (The word separation varies from one search engine to another.) Some search engines allow you to specify the word separation by placing a / (front or right slash) followed by a number after the NEAR (NEAR/30 means to search for your search criteria up to 30 words apart).

"Toyota Corolla 2003" - use of " " (quotes) for a phrase will limit your search result to text that matches the information in the exact order of the text between the quotes. If an article contained Toyota Corolla, you would not see it because it did not have 2003. If the information in the article said 2003 Toyota Corolla you would not see that either because it is out of order.

Toyota Coro* - use the " * " (asterisk) if you are not sure of the spelling of a word or the word may have multiple endings. Your search results will show you all articles that have Toyota and the first four letters Coro. It may come back with words like Corolla, coro, El Coro, Corona or other words that use the same letters. It can also be used as a wildcard.

"Toyota and 2003" **Not** Corolla - This will show you all Toyotas that have 2003 in the article but it will leave out articles that contain Corolla.

Sporty AND (Toyota AND 2003 OR 2004) - use of "( )" parentheses will search for all articles that contain Toyota along with 2003 or 2004 and then it will give you the results of the ones that also contain the Sporty in the text. Parentheses allow you to build complex searches and specify in which order it should occur (items in the parentheses are completed first) If you use a combination of the operator words (AND, OR and NOT) they will automatically be selected in the following order: NOT,

AND, OR no matter what order you typed them in unless you use parentheses.

The following tips can help you out: be as specific as possible, ensure spelling is correct, use similar terms if you do not get matches on your search, use as many words as possible to narrow your search, do not use ed, ing, or s on the end of words, do not capitalize unless it is absolutely necessary, ignore small words like of, the, a, and.

The nice thing about most of these commands is they can be mixed with other commands to create searches that are even more refined. Understanding how to perform these searches will make the Internet a very powerful tool at your fingertips. I hope this will make it a bit easier to take advantage of the vast amount of information available to us all. Many menus online can help you with searching. Just search on "internet search commands" or "search engines."

Other Tips

➢ If you smoke a pack of cigarettes a day and stop smoking, you would save $3.50 or more per day. If you invested that money at 5 percent, in 20 years you would have over $43,300.00. It may even save your life.

➢ Many women still pay a lot more for haircuts. Ask why the men's haircuts are cheaper than for the women. Many women nowadays have short hair, and many men have long hair. You need to speak out and spread the word.

➢ Do not waste money on lottery tickets, or cut back on the amount you buy.

➢ If you are sending an E-mail to someone you have not dealt with before and are looking for a quick response try to put the words "Second Notice" in your subject line. That seems to get people to be more responsive.

➤ Do you buy a lot of CD's (Compact Discs)? Consider downloading the music from some of the free Web sites. You can also buy CD's used, or purchase a trade in, at some stores.

➤ Do you really need premium cable, pay as you go movie channels, or cable TV? If you save $12.00 a month and invest it at 5% interest, in 10 years you will save over $1,800.00.

➤ If you like to go to the movies, it may be cheaper to rent a video. By the time you add up all the extra costs for popcorn, drinks, etc., it becomes very expensive for a family of four to go to the theater.

➤ Do you really need a cell phone or all of the extra features you have on your home phone? If you have Internet service, look for a cheaper provider. Some are free while others only charge $9.95 a month. If you can save $10.00 per month and invest it at 5 percent for 20 years, you will save over $4,000.00.

➤ Always keep your eye on your drink at a party, bar, etc. Someone could spike your drink when you are not looking (date rape drugs, etc.).

➤ Ask stores, restaurants, pharmacies, banks, etc. if they offer senior citizen discounts.

➤ It seems that many of us tend to delay doing things that need to be done. We have the time to get something done yet we say that we will get to it another day. Then something else happens and you say that you will get to it later. Stop procrastinating and take care of things before it is too late or the problem becomes worse.

➢ Do not use features like "*69" on your home phone to dial the last person that called you. The cost is not worth the convenience of calling someone back. If it was important, they will call you back. If you are using it because you are receiving harassment calls, check with your phone company for other options. In that case it may be worth the cost.

➢ Look up the phone number yourself and save the directory assistance charges.

➢ If you want to buy a boat, RV, or cabin in the woods, consider renting first to see if you like it. It may be cheaper to rent it altogether if you do not plan to use it frequently.

➢ Prevent a shaken carbonated soda can from exploding when you open it. Tap on the can for 20 seconds before opening to dislodge CO_2 bubbles from the bottom and sides of the can.

➢ Keep the icing from sticking to the wrapper on flat-topped cupcakes. Turn the package of cupcakes upside down on a flat surface, apply medium pressure, and slide them back and forth about 10 times. Open carefully, peeling the wrapper off slowly.

➢ Have you had more children than you planned for or just do not want any more. Consider having a vasectomy (man) or tubal ligation (woman). Accidents do happen.

➢ If you are in need of a lawyer, seek one that specializes in the field that you need help with (criminal, copyright, real estate, trusts, power of attorney, personal injury, etc.).

➢ I feel that everybody should get out and vote because we can all make a difference in the way our government functions. Many people believe that their vote will not count. Just think of how many other people are thinking the same thing. These numbers are very high and those votes can easily sway an election. There are other good reasons to vote. Sometime in your life you may need some type of help with health related issues, need a job, resolve a traffic violation, etc. If you are a registered voter, you can go to your party's committee member and request assistance.

➢ Do you receive lots of junk E-mail messages from telemarketers or people you do not know? If you find this unsolicited commercial E-mail - also known as "spam" - annoying and time consuming, reply back to the site. Ask them to remove your name and E-mail address from their distribution list and to not send you any future E-mails. If a Web site does not honor your request then you can file a complaint with the FTC (Federal Trade Commission). Follow these steps to track down spammers and trace their Internet domain in the E-mail address.

Go to www.Network-tools.com
Select "Xwhois"
Search and enter the domain name.
Once you have that information, report the spammer's information to your Internet provider or FTC.
www.FTC.gov/spam

➢ When you go to the hairdresser do not let them use hair conditioner after he/she washes your hair if they charge extra for it. You can do that the next time you wash your hair. Be wary of all the extra charges that can add up.

➢ Do you ever have one of those days when you feel everything is going wrong, or you just feel down? Our minds are always wandering and we seem to focus on negative issues. Instead, focus on something you like to do or enjoy. Just keep thinking about it and your negative thoughts will fade away. You can control what your mind is thinking. Think positively and you will perform better throughout the day.

> This statement will probably get me into trouble, but as much as I would like to think that men are better than women at many trades, that is not quite true. I have noticed that if a man and a woman have the same opportunities in training, the woman tends to have more knowledge on the job. It may not be the knowledge, but they seem to listen and understand things better. They do not tend to be as quick to respond negatively as a man. What does all this mean? If you take your car to a mechanic, do not necessarily choose the man over the woman. Alternatively, if you have to see a doctor, you may want to choose the woman because she will probably listen to what you have to say. Just think about some of your past experiences and you be the judge. Again, that is my manly opinion.

> Take cans of soda to work instead of buying soda during the day. Just think of the savings over time, 25 cents or less versus $1.00 per day, if you only buy one. Do not always buy lunch, bring it from home. You need to do the math with everything. If you take the $3.75 you save each week by bringing your soda, and invest it at 5 percent, for 15 years, you will save over $4,300.00.

> Are you tired of those annoying telemarketing calls? You are sitting at dinner and the phone rings. It seems that all of the telemarketers decided to call you that night. All we want is a little privacy in our home. In most cases, you can now get it. Check with your state's Attorney General Office to see if they have the "DO NOT CALL" law program in your area. You can usually register your name at your local Attorney General Web site. Add each of your phone numbers to the list. It usually takes a few months for it to take effect. As of the printing of this book, it is a free service.

> You can also contact The Direct Marketing Association's (The DMA) Telephone Preference Service (TPS), a do-

not-call service. This is a service to assist those consumers in decreasing the number of national commercial calls received at home. You can register via mail for free or online and pay a $5.00 processing fee for registering with TPS service.

To register by mail, send a signed letter with the following information: name, address, phone number to:

> DMA Telephone Preference Service
> PO Box 1559
> Carmel, NY 10512

To register online, visit www.dmaconsumers.org.
You must register your name, address, and phone number with TPS directly; third party requests cannot be processed.

Or you could add a small electronic device, called a Telezapper, to your phone line. It will eliminate most of your calls over time. It works on computer-dialed telemarketing calls by sending a signal indicating your phone number has been disconnected. This product will not stop people that manually dial the phone. It is a good alternative. You will need one Telezapper for each phone line that you want to protect.

➤ Instead of sending letters in the mail, use the Internet and send them as an E-mail attachment. If you are not sure how to do it, just ask any teenager. That is how I found out. It will not only save you money, but it will arrive within seconds of being sent.

➤ If you feel uncomfortable about negotiating, returning items to the store, or registering complaints, try this: I tell the person that my spouse or mother is not happy and I have to do it because of them. Most of the time they just feel sorry for me.

➢ Save *UPC codes* from boxes. If a company has promotions, rebates, or contests, you already have what you need.

➢ If you go out to restaurants, consider cutting back or eating at less expensive ones.

➢ Many people like the convenience of taking their clothes to the dry-cleaner. Read the labels. Most clothes today do not have to be dry-cleaned. Those costs can add up very quickly. If you save $10.00 per week by not dry-cleaning, and you invest your savings at 5 percent over 20 years, you would end up with over $17,600.00.

➢ We should all be careful when reading or listening to advertisements. Many people believe everything they hear because they want it to be true. Then they end up spending money on things they do not need or that do not work as advertised.

Throughout this chapter I have given you many ideas to save money. In some cases I have provided some actual numbers so you can see the impact of those suggestions. The five percent investment rate that I used, along with many other numbers, was very conservative. The more you make in your investments, the larger your savings will be.

As you can see, you could easily reach your goals with some minor changes in your lifestyle. I am not saying to go right out and make all of these changes at once. Pick two items a week from the book, or another idea that you may have. Start with the ones that will save you the most. Invest the money you save, or add it to a mortgage, loan, or credit card payment to get the most out of it. Remember you may be saying that the book has many great ideas. However, they are not great unless you follow through and start applying these skills.

Beware of bad tips that can cost you money, time, and aggravation. Remember the old saying that "if it sounds too good to be true, it usually is." Below are just a few things to remember.

- Do not reveal passwords or a PIN (Personal Identification Number) to anyone.
- Keep track of bills and statements. If you notice unusual charges report them to the company immediately.
- When leasing a car, be sure to read the entire lease agreement before signing. Some agreements include life insurance as part of your payment. You should cross it out or reword it if you do not want it. Both parties must initial before signing. Always read the fine print.
- Those of us who have Internet access are always receiving Spam (junk E-mail). Keep an open mind for hoaxes that try to mislead you. Stay away from chain letters. Do not panic if you see messages or E-mails that warn you about viruses. But do scan outside messages with virus detection software before opening.
- Do not fall for those get rich quick businesses, or where you have to pay small deposits, or pay for a class. Do not put money into anything that says you will make a lot of money quickly without any real work.

Some of the most important things that will make you successful using these skills are:

- Do not let the people you are dealing with intimidate you.
- Be sure to stand up for your rights.
- If you strongly believe in something, follow it through no matter how impossible you may think it is to accomplish.
- If you are not satisfied with the results, do something about it.
- Do not be afraid to ask for something.
- Do not believe everything you are told. Verify and re-verify if necessary.
- Speak up when necessary.
- Treat others the way you expect to be treated.

If you are in business or plan to go into business, remember the following things.

- Treat the customer as if he/she is right even though they may be wrong.
- Always treat the customer with respect.
- Always let them finish speaking without interruption.
- Listen carefully to what they have to say.
- If they leave a message, respond back to them quickly, even though you may not have an answer for them.
- Let them know when you will get back to them and make sure you follow through with that promise.
- Always remember the things you did to get your business started. Do not change once you become successful.
- Continue to treat people equally even though you have reached your plateau of success.
- And, of course, stand behind your product or service.

I would like to end this book with a few things to think about. It is not all about making or saving money. Many things cause us aggravation and stress in our daily lives. Do these things happen to you?

- You are in a traffic jam with nowhere to go, and the person behind you blows their horn.
- You try to get off the elevator and others rush in before you can get off, or they just block the path.
- You are nice to hold the door for someone walking in behind you and everyone else suddenly feels that you should be the door attendant, rather than taking the door from you, or even thanking you.
- The person in front of you in the left lane is traveling the speed limit. You and others must go around them by moving to the right lane that has been clear for a while.
- You open the door for a family member and suddenly others push their way in, and your family member is still outside the door.

- You are on a crowded bus where everyone is sitting except some senior citizen who is standing and trying to hold on to the rail and his/her bags at the same time.
- Someone cuts right in front of you as they turn from a side street. There was no traffic at all behind you. Now they are driving below the speed limit.
- You are going for the door and the person in front of you lets it close on you before you even had a chance to grab the handle.
- The person in front of you is driving slowly and recklessly while talking on his/her cell phone.
- The person in front of you moves into your lane without tuning on their turn signal. They are so close that you feel you could reach out and touch the vehicle, which is traveling at 60 mph.
- You see someone doing something suspicious, but you do not get involved. You think that the next person will do something about it.
- You are patiently waiting in your vehicle to get off at an exit that is backed up for a mile. Others keep cutting in front of you almost causing an accident each time.
- You are in a movie and the person sitting next to you is talking on his/her cell phone.
- You are traveling in a school zone at 15 mph and the person behind you is right on your bumper.
- You are in a meeting and someone comes in late and expects to be informed while others are waiting.

Above are just a few examples of aggravation caused by others in our daily lives. We have all been in these situations at one time or another. In some cases, we are the ones that cause the aggravation for the other person and ourselves. Most of these acts of rudeness only save us a few seconds of our time. In some cases we are putting our own lives and others at risk by tailing people or cutting them off. Is it worth the few seconds knowing that it may be causing an impact to someone else's life? Think of things that you may have done wrong and try not to repeat them in the future. Think of the things you have done that help others and do them more often. If we all do this, the world would become less aggravating for all of us. Let us make this a better world. We can definitely make it happen. None of us are perfect, myself included.

I hope you found this book as interesting to read as I found it to write. As I sat down and gathered all of my thoughts, I soon came to realize that I had forgotten many of these things myself. As the list kept getting longer, I knew that this book was going to be a success because of the helpful information in it. In many cases, I have learned through trial and error. And let me tell you there were many errors and costly mistakes in my life. I hope that you have bought this book at a young age and you start to take advantage of these tips immediately. And for those who have made some of these same mistakes, this book will hopefully steer you in the right direction in the future. Either way I realized I needed a book just for me. I hope you can get the benefits that I have realized over the years. I will personally give a copy to my lovely wife and daughter who will benefit from it for the rest of their lives. Good luck and many successes now and in the future.

References

U.S. Department Of Energy
U.S. Environmental Protection Agency

Glossary

airbag (SRS) - a device part of the passive safety system. Sensors cause the airbag to inflate in the event of an accident. Your head is then cushioned by the bag instead of hitting the dashboard or steering wheel.

alternative container - a plain unfinished wood or non-metal box that is generally lower in cost than a casket.

Annual Fuel Utilization Efficiency (AFUE) - is a measurement of how efficient an appliance is in using fossil fuel (gas or oil) or electricity (for an electric furnace) over a typical year of use.

antilock brake system (ABS) - a device which senses that one or more of the wheels are locking up during braking. It is controlled by both mechanical and electronic components to brake rapidly and alternate from full pressure to full release. Both maximum braking and maximum steering control is allowed during braking with the use of ABS. Never pump the brakes if you have ABS.

authorized dealer - a manufacturer's representative authorized to sell an item or service to a consumer or other retailer for resale.

automated teller machine (ATM) - a machine that is generally located outside of a bank that dispenses cash when a personal coded card is used.

backorder - sold out item that will be in stock within a certain number of days.

basin - a natural depression in the surface of the land often with water at the bottom of it.

bottom line - slang term for net income or profit made.

broker - a person whose business is to negotiate selling insurance on another's behalf and represents multiple companies.

browser - a program that is used to access documents on the Internet.

bumper-to-bumper - a way of expressing the entire vehicle from one bumper to the other.

carbon monoxide - an odorless, colorless, tasteless, and toxic gas produced as a by-product of combustion. Any fuel-burning appliance, vehicle, tool, or other device has the potential to produce dangerous levels of *carbon monoxide* gas.

carbon monoxide detector - a device used to sense Carbon Monoxide toxicity levels.

carbon monoxide exposure - Compounding the effects of the exposure is its long half-life of carboxyhemoglobin (COHb) in the blood. Half-life is a measure by how quickly levels return to normal. The half-life of COHb is approximately 5 hours. This means that for a given exposure level, it will take about 5 hours for the level of COHb in the blood to drop to half its current level after the exposure is terminated. The following symptoms are associated with CO toxicity. They are expressed in airborne concentration levels Parts Per Million (PPM) and duration of exposure.

PPM CO	Time	Symptoms *
0 PPM		Desirable.
9 PPM		Maximum acceptable level of CO in a living space.
35 PPM	8 hours	Maximum exposure allowed by OSHA in the workplace over an eight-hour period.
200 PPM	2-3 hours	Mild headache, fatigue, nausea and dizziness.
400 PPM	1-2 hours	Serious headache – other

		symptoms intensify. Life threatening after 3 hours.
800 PPM	45 minutes	Dizziness, nausea and convulsions. Unconscious. within 2 hours. Death within 2-3 hours.
1600 PPM	20 minutes	Headache, dizziness and. nausea. Death within 1 hour.
3200 PPM	5-10 minutes	Headache, dizziness and nausea. Death within 1 hour.
6400 PPM	1-2 minutes	Headache, dizziness and nausea. Death within 25-30 minutes.
12,800 PPM	1-3 minutes	Death.

* Symptoms can vary significantly. It depends on many factors such as weight, health, unborn baby, sex, pregnant women, age, etc.

casket - a box or chest made of wood, metal or plastic into which the deceased is placed for burial. Sometimes referred to as "coffin" or "burial case."

cemetery property - an area of ground set aside for burial or *entombment* of the deceased in a grave, crypt, or *niche*.

cemetery services - opening and closing graves, crypts, or niches; setting grave liners and vaults; setting markers; and long-term maintenance of cemetery grounds and facilities.

Chief Executive Officer (CEO) - title often held by the chairperson of the board, or the president. The person who is principally responsible for the activities of the company.

collect call - a telephone call that the receiving party is asked to pay for.

columbarium - a structure with small spaces for placing cremated remains in urns or other approved containers.

commission - a payment system based on a percentage of the value of sales.

competitors - other companies with which the original company competes for business.

compulsive - the recurrent failure to resist the impulse to buy unneeded objects.

confirm - to give new assurance of the truth of; to render certain; to verify; to corroborate; as, to confirm a price.

coniferous - a cone bearing evergreen tree or shrub with needle-type leaves such as a spruce, fir, cedar, pine, yew, etc.

contour line - is a line symbol, which joins points of equal elevation above sea level.

cremation - process which reduces the body by heat to small bone fragments, which are pulverized reducing them to the consistency of coarse sand or crushed seashells.

crypt - a space in a mausoleum or other building to hold cremated or whole remains.

dealer invoice - the price the dealer pays for a vehicle.

deciduous - perennial plants that are normally leafless for some time during the year.

deductible - an amount that a policyholder agrees to pay, per claim or per accident, toward the total amount of an insured loss.

demo - a product used for demonstration and often sold later at a discount.

department - a division of a business specializing in a particular product or service.

direct burial - the deceased is buried shortly after death, usually in a simple container. No viewing or visitation is involved, so no embalming is necessary. A memorial service may be held at the graveside or later. This type of burial usually costs less than the traditional. Costs include the funeral home's basic services fee, as well as transportation and care of the body, the purchase of a casket or burial container and a cemetery plot or crypt. If the family chooses to be at the cemetery for the burial, the funeral home often charges an additional fee for a graveside service.

direct cremation - the deceased is cremated shortly after death, without embalming. The cremated remains are placed in an urn or other container. No viewing or visitation is involved, although a memorial service may be held, with or without the cremated remains present. The remains can be kept in the home, buried or placed in a crypt or niche in a cemetery, or buried or scattered in a favorite spot. Direct cremation usually costs less than the traditional funeral. Costs include the funeral home's basic services fee, as well as transportation and care of the body. A crematory fee may be included or, if the funeral home does not own the crematory, the fee may be added on. There also will be a charge for an urn or other container. The cost of a cemetery plot or crypt is included only if the remains are buried or entombed.

director - one who directs; one who regulates, guides, or orders; a manager.

Direct Purchase Plan (DPP) - A Securities and Exchange Commission (SEC) regulated program that enables companies to sell shares of stock directly to investors. This allows the investor to not pay brokerage or commission fees. Also referred to as direct participation program (DPP) and direct stock purchase plan (DSPP).

disposition - the final resting place for the body or for cremated remains. Choices include burial of the body in the earth or a mausoleum; burial, scattering or deposit of cremated remains in an urn for placement in a niche or taking home; donation of the body to a research facility or burial at sea.

Dividend Reinvestment Plan (DRIP) - An investment plan offered by some companies enabling shareholders to automatically reinvest dividends and capital gains.

They can accumulate more stock without paying brokerage or commission fees.

easement - a right of passage over one's land or waterway. Easements are also classified as negative (it prevents the landowner from doing certain things) or affirmative easements (the most common, which allows the beneficiary of the easement to do certain things, such as a right-of-way).

efficiency - operating or performing in an effective and competent manner, with little wasted effort.

electronic ignition - an ignition system using electronic switching devices to assist or eliminate the use of a constant flame.

elevation - the height of a point on the earth's surface relative to mean sea level (msl).

E-mail - the exchange of computer-stored messages by telecommunication.

embalming - a cosmetic enhancement, designed to last for a few days after the funeral and burial, in which the deceased is treated with antiseptics and preservatives.

Endowment Care Fund - money collected from *cemetery property* purchasers and placed in trust for the maintenance and upkeep of the cemetery.

Energy Efficiency Rating (EER) - a measurement of how much energy it will take to do a specific amount of cooling. The higher the EER number, the more efficient the unit and the greater the money saved.
Here is an easy formula:

$$\frac{\text{Air Conditioner Cooling Output (BTU Rating)}}{\text{Air Conditioner Electricity Input (Watts Rating)}} = (EER)$$

Glossary

Energy Factor (EF) - the measurement of the overall efficiency for different appliances. For water heaters, the energy factor is based on following factors: the recovery efficiency, or how efficiently the heat from the energy source is transferred to the water, the percentage of heat lost per hour from the stored water compared to the heat content of the water, and cycling losses. For dishwashers, the energy factor is defined as the number of cycles per kWh of input power. For clothes washers, the energy factor is defined as the cubic foot capacity per kWh of input power per cycle. For clothes dryers, the energy factor is defined as the number of pounds of clothes dried per kWh of power consumed.

entombment - placement of the body in a casket above ground in a mausoleum.

escrow account - an account that the lender or mortgage servicer establishes to hold funds for the payments for property taxes and insurance.

Expected Family Contribution (EFC) - a calculation representing the amount of money that a student and his or her parents will be expected to contribute to education costs in a given year. It takes many factors in consideration including geographical location.

extended warranty - many confuse this with the manufactures warranty, but it has nothing to do with the original manufacturer's vehicles warranty. This contract is between the warranty company and you. They pay you for repairs covered by the contract. These contracts are insured by a third party in case the warranty company goes out of business.

fair market value - the amount for which property would sell on the open market if put up for sale. This is distinguished from "replacement value," which is the cost of duplicating the property. Real estate appraisers will use "comparable" sales of similar property in the area to determine market value, adding or deducting amounts based on differences in quality and size of the property.

federal aid - money provided to a student and/or his or her family to help pay for the student's education. It can be in the form of gift aid (grants and scholarships) or self-help aid (loans and work-study).

FICO score (Fair, Isaac and Company) - is a credit-risk scoring system that was developed by Fair, Isaac, for use by the three national credit bureaus. Each credit bureau produces Fico scores under a different brand name for use by business to check credit ratings and approve loans. The Fico score is a three-digit number mathematically calculated from credit history information in a person's credit report. The score predicts the likelihood that the person will pay back borrowed money as agreed during the next two years. The score considers the following information from your credit report: have you paid your bills on time, how much do you currently owe creditors, how long have you handled credit, what types of credit have you handled, and are you taking on more debt. Fico scores range from 150 to 950, with half of all consumers scoring 720 or higher. The higher the number, the better your chances are for getting loan approval and lower interest rates.

flue damper - a valve, usually a moveable or rotatable plate, for controlling the flow of air or smoke and draft in a fireplace.

fluorescent bulb - in a fluorescent bulb, electricity is used to excite gas within the bulb. This gas emits radiation, which is absorbed by phosphor on the walls of the bulb. The phosphor in turn emits visible light.

footprint - the amount of space any particular unit of hardware occupies.

Glossary

401K - a retirement investment plan that allows an employee to put a percentage of earned wages into a tax-deferred investment account selected by the employer.

funeral ceremony - a service honoring the deceased, with the body present.

funeral services - 1)services provided by a funeral director and staff, which may include consulting with the family on funeral planning; transportation, shelter, refrigeration and embalming of remains; preparing and filing notices; obtaining authorizations and permits; and coordinating with the cemetery, crematory or other third parties. 2) The religious or other rites conducted immediately before final disposition of the dead human body.

gasketed - also known as "protective" or "sealer" caskets. These terms mean that the casket has a rubber gasket or some other feature that is designed to delay the penetration of water into the casket and prevent rust.

general manager (GM) - the highest ranking manager.

grates - a structure of metal bars that covers an opening.

grave - an excavation in the earth for the purpose of burying the remains.

grave liner - a concrete cover that fits over the casket. Some liners cover tops and sides of the casket. This is required by most cemeteries to prevent the collapse and ground settling after burial. State law, however, usually does not require a grave liner. Also referred to as the "outer container."

graveside service - formal committal services conducted at the cemetery.

gray unit - when genuinely branded merchandise flows through unauthorized channels. The distribution usually takes place across market borders, where environmental conditions are conducive to profits. Gray marketers are generally distributors that capitalize on price differentials via the purchase of goods in one market, either from an authorized dealer or directly from the manufacturer and then re-sell the product in a higher-priced market at a profit. Many times the merchandise is not built to the required specifications for the market that it is being sold in.

guarantee - a promise or an assurance, especially one given in writing, that attests to the quality or durability of a product or service.

Guaranteed Auto Protection (GAP) - as your car's value depreciates, your loan/lease balance may be significantly higher. If your car were stolen, or totaled in an accident, you would be liable to pay the difference between your insurance settlement and your outstanding loan/lease balance. GAP insurance pays the difference between what you owe on your vehicle and what your insurance covers.

headquarters - the office that serves as the administrative center of an enterprise.

Heating Seasonal Performance Factor (HSPF) - a representation of the total heating output of a central air-conditioning heat pump in BTUs during its normal usage period for heating, divided by the total electrical energy input in watt-hours during the same period, as determined using the specified test procedures. Efficiency is derived according to federal test methods by using the total Btu's during its normal usage period for heating divided by the total electrical energy input in watt-hours during the same period.

house wrap - a material that seals the gaps and cracks which helps the insulation of the inside walls. It protects against air infiltration, manages moisture vapor, and protects the wall when rain and water get behind siding or brick. It increases the *R-Value* and helps reduce energy bills.

Glossary

incandescent bulb - This most common type of bulb uses electricity to heat a filament until it glows and illuminates the area around it.

infrared camera - is a non-contact device that detects infrared energy (heat) and converts it into an electronic signal, which is then processed to produce a thermal image on a video monitor and perform temperature calculations. Heat sensed by an infrared camera can be very precisely quantified, or measured, allowing you to not only monitor thermal performance, but also identify and evaluate the relative severity of heat-related problems.

insulate - to cover or surround something with a material or substance in order to stop heat from escaping or entering.

interment - burial in the ground, *inurnment,* or entombment.

Internet - a large system of many connected computers around the world, which people use to communicate with each other.

inurnment - the placing of cremated remains in an urn.

inventory - items that are either available for sale or are being prepared for sale.

karat - the unit of measurement for the proportion of gold in an alloy; 18-karat gold is 75% gold; 24-karat gold is pure gold.

kilowatt-hours (kWh) - a unit of electric energy equivalent to the work done by one kilowatt acting for one hour.

lowball - to deliberately underestimate or understate the cost

Low-E glass - low emissivity glass is made with an invisible coating on the glass that blocks solar radiation and heat flow. Heat always flows towards cold. In the winter, heat from the inside flows to the outside. In the summer, the outside heat flows in toward the cooler interior. This coating helps to reflect heat back to the inside in winter and outside in the summer.

lumens - the unit of luminous flux in the International System, equal to the amount of light given out through a solid angle by a source of one candela intensity radiating equally in all directions.

market value - price at which real estate could presumably be purchased or sold for.

markup - an amount added to a cost price in calculating a selling price, especially an amount that takes into account overhead and profit.

mausoleum - a large stately tomb or a building housing such a tomb or several tombs in which remains are buried or entombed.

memorial service - a ceremony honoring the deceased, without the remains being present.

Modified Energy Factor (MEF) - is a combination of Energy Factor and Remaining Moisture Content. MEF measures energy consumption of the total laundry cycle (washing and drying). It indicates how many cubic feet of laundry can be washed and dried with one kWh of electricity; the higher the number, the greater the efficiency.

motion sensor - these are active sensors that inject energy (light, microwaves, or sound) into the environment in order to detect a change of some sort.

niche - a shell-like space in a wall made for the placing of urns containing cremated remains, or inside a building for this purpose, which is called a columbarium. Urns are placed in these niches as a final resting place for cremated remains.

OP meter (off-peak meter) - commonly referred to as load management. A power provider that allows specific loads to be turned off during periods of peak electrical demand. Connecting to a separate meter that bills usage at a reduced rate usually does this.

policy - a plan or course of action, as of business, intended to influence and determine decisions, actions, and other matters.

premise burglar alarm - is a proprietary burglar alarm system that has alarm initiating circuits and devices, which are installed at a property and are connected directly or indirectly to constantly monitored receiving central supervising station. The system is arranged so that a pre-determined change in the alarm initiating circuits or devices automatically causes transmission of an alarm signal over a supervised signaling channel to the central supervising station.

price match - if you find the identical item in another competitor's store, current newspaper, catalog, or Website, simply provide verifiable proof of where you saw the merchandise and they will lower the selling price.

Private Mortgage Insurance (PMI) - insurance provided by a non-government insurer that protects a lender against loss if the borrower defaults.

profit - the return received on a business undertaking after all operating expenses have been met.

property tax appeal - a complaint with respect to the current value assessment of your property.

restrictions - to limit the movements or actions of someone, or to limit something and reduce its size or prevent it from increasing.

retail - the activity of selling goods to the public, usually in small quantities. (As opposed to a dealers or brokers.)

revoke - to say officially that an agreement, permission, or law is no longer effective.

R-Value - A unit of thermal resistance used to measure the effectiveness of insulation. A higher R-value number indicates better insulating properties in material.

Seasonal Energy Efficiency Rating (SEER) - is the efficiency rating for air conditioning units. The higher the SEER rating, the better the energy efficiency. SEER is the ratio of the amount of BTUs used for cooling in normal annual use to the total amount of electrical power (measured in watts) over the same period. (Annual Cooling in BTU's/Total Watt Hours = SEER).

scholarship - a grant of financial aid awarded to a student, for the purpose of attending college. One is generally made, based on an applicant meeting certain eligibility criteria.

solar heat gain coefficient (SHGC) - measures how well a product blocks heat caused by sunlight. The lower a window's SHGC, the less solar heat it transmits.

sticker price - the list price for a vehicle.

suspend - to debar, or cause to withdraw temporarily, from any privilege.

swale - an artificial depression excavated to carry water across land during times of rainfall.

traditional - a type of funeral, often referred to by funeral providers as a full service funeral, usually includes a viewing or visitation and formal funeral service, use of a hearse to transport the body to the funeral site and cemetery, and burial, entombment or cremation of the remains. It is generally the most expensive type of funeral. In addition to the funeral home's basic services fee, costs often include embalming and dressing the body; rental of the funeral home for the viewing or service; and use of vehicles to transport the family if they don't use their own.

Glossary

UPC code - a bar code symbol that encodes twelve-digits. A number is assigned to a product and six of the digits identify the manufacturer's assigned number.

Urn - a container to hold cremated remains. They are made from various materials including wood, marble or metal. It can be placed in a columbarium or mausoleum, or buried in the ground.

U-value - a measure of the heat transmission through a building part (as a wall or window) or a given thickness of a material (as insulation) with lower numbers indicating better insulating properties.

vault - a grave liner that completely encloses a casket, which is partly or fully underground.

vice president (VP) - A deputy to a president, especially in a corporation, in charge of a specific department or location.

voicemail - an interactive computerized system for answering and routing telephone calls, for recording, saving, and relaying messages, and sometimes for paging the user.

warranty - a guarantee by a seller to a buyer that if a product requires repair or remedy of a problem within a certain period after its purchase, the seller will repair the problem at no cost to the buyer.

Web - also known as WWW, is the graphical multimedia aspect of the Internet. It comprises content, with the basic language of HTML and a *browser*. The content resides on a Web server.

wholesale - the activity of selling goods to businesses, which then sell them to the public.

window etching - a 20-minute process that involves chemically etching car windows with the vehicle identification number. This often results in a reduction of insurance cost.

Index

Index

Index

Index

Index

See What Others are Saying about the Author

Mike taught me to always negotiate for the best prices with decision makers and he taught me how to save money. For example, Mike taught me how to research the dealer price of a car so I can negotiate better with the car dealer. I was able to save an extra 10% on my new car. Mike also gave me tips such as using my student ID to save 90% on tickets to concerts.

- Noel Abejo, Philadelphia, PA

I was looking to buy a new car and I visited several dealers in the area and got my best price. I thought it was good deal. The agreement I had made with the dealership included a 60,000 mile warranty at no cost. I then approached Mr. Ellenbogen in hopes of his assistance, already knowing of his previous successes in acquiring the best deals. I spoke with Mr. Ellenbogen to let him know and he told me he could save me another thousand off the price. When Mr. Ellenbogen was finished he had brought the price down by a thousand dollars, as he expected, and I now had a 100,000 mile warranty at no cost to myself.

- Odette Barnett, Sunrise, FL

I read your book on money saving ideas and I saved a bundle. I can't thank you enough.

Last month I took on the painstaking challenge of buying a new car. I'm not much of a negotiator and dread the dealer visit. But after reading your chapter on how to buy a car, I was armed with knowledge. I first decided on the make and model of the car I wanted. I used the internet to search and decide on my next vehicle. I then contacted several of the car dealers in the buying area and told them what I wanted. It was great. Each dealer was almost begging for my business. As I got one estimate I told the next dealer and asked if they could beat it. It only took about a week and I finally had about two good choices. I decided on the dealer closest to me and visited them that night. Most of the work was already done. The back and forth negotiations were eliminated. I signed that night and drove home a brand new car. My final price was several hundreds less than invoice.

I can't wait to read the next chapter. Thanks again.

- Steve Liesner, Newtown, PA

ISBN 1-41206185-7